G

THE ARCHITECTURE OF ITALY

The Architecture of Italy

DOREEN YARWOOD

Harper & Row, Publishers

NEW YORK and EVANSTON

Contents

1589873

Plates

Preface

THE Italian fine arts, painting, and sculpture especially, are well represented in the books available at the moment. Most of these books are pictorial, containing quality as well as a quantity of reproductive illustration. There is also illustrative material available of Italian architecture in text books on certain limited periods, notably the Renaissance and Baroque. Very little exists in the English language of the history and development of the whole canvas of this subject and both tourists and students often ask 'what is the difference between Roman, Renaissance and Baroque buildings in Italy' or 'what is Byzantine architecture and why is it different in Italy from that in Greece or Turkey'.

The aim of this book is to provide an introduction to the complete field of architectural development in the Italian peninsula, treated chronologically from its days as a Greek colony in the 6th century B.C. to the present time. The book has been planned to provide suitable material for students and it is

hoped that it will also appeal to the growing numbers of tourists visiting Italy for the first or even 20th time who wish to know something of its architecture and of why it developed in this way.

Emphasis has been given to the most interesting and vital periods of architecture in Italy: those of Ancient Rome, Romanesque, the Renaissance, Baroque. More than half the space has been given to illustration in order to make recognition easy. The text presents a general outline of how styles evolved, the reasons behind this at the time and comparison with and cross-reference to equivalent English development.

I should like to express my appreciation of the generous help given by Prof. Dott. Maria A. Lorriman in advising on general data in Italy and matters pertaining to the Italian language. I should also like to thank my husband for taking over 2,000 photographs in Italy from which the drawings have been made. We have visited and studied all the buildings illustrated and referred to in the book.

DOREEN YARWOOD

PART ONE

Ancient Greece and Rome

CHAPTER 1

Greek 6th Century B.C. to 146 B.C.

THE remains of Greek architecture in Italy are not numerous though the buildings are more complete than those to be found elsewhere in the world. It is appropriate, however, to discuss and illustrate the comparative construction of all classical architecture in the peninsula. This is because in Italy, more than in any other country, the classical form provided the basis and pattern for some 80 per cent of all buildings created during the last 2500 years. While northern Europe was designing in Medieval style, the Italians were still strongly influenced by the classical tradition. The ties with ancient Rome were long lasting, extending into the early Middle Ages and, at the latter end, the Renaissance began here earlier than anywhere else in Europe, so restarting classical design. Even in the 20th century, with post-war contemporary materials and construction, the Italians are still sometimes thought not to have broken entirely with their classical past even though (or perhaps because of this) their modern work has been so outstandingly successful.

It is simpler, therefore, to begin by discussing these classical precepts in general, then, in each succeeding and varying period of classical form, reference can be made to the original sources. Pages 8 and 9 are laid out to show, in comparative manner, the orders, ornament, mouldings and construction from the Greek mainland, from Greek remains in Italy, from Ancient Rome and from Italian Renaissance and Baroque examples. On page 12 are shown drawings of extant remains in Italy.

The Greeks established the *classical* form of architecture, the Romans adapted it to their needs and Italian Renaissance architects rediscovered and further altered it to the requirements of their day.

It is thus Greek remains which should be studied first in order to trace the architectural development. All such remains are ruined: the roofs have gone, so light enters where the forms were designed for shade thus altering the balance of the three-dimensional design; the sculpture and much of the decoration have been taken away to museums; the colour which once vividly covered much of the buildings has weathered away and all the metal and wood parts have vanished. It is thus a tribute to the greatness of perfection in Greek architectural design that these ruins should give such aesthetic satisfaction to the modern traveller. This beauty derives not from variation in form but from quality of line and proportion which had resulted from centuries of study and experience. The Greek Hellenic building style emerged from an archaic period lasting from about 700–480 B.C. to its zenith of great achievement in the 5th and 4th centuries B.C., continuing in similar manner until the Roman Conquest in 146 B.C. The construction was a *trabeated* one—a word evolving from the Latin *trabes*, meaning a beam. It is also called the post-and-lintel type of construction. It consists of vertical members (columns) supporting horizontal beams (marble blocks). With the development of a lintel stone carried on two verticals to form an opening, followed the full glory of temple colonnades, which are simply an extension of the principle. In Greece the climate made an open air life desirable and such colonnades provided shade, shelter and fresh air.

Greek buildings included temples, theatres, market places (*agora*) with shops, town fortifications and treasuries. Most of the remains are of temples and theatres, though the latter have been altered by later Roman usage. The domains of Ancient Greece

7

THE FUNDAMENTALS OF CLASSICAL ARCHITECTURE:

1. GREEK DORIC.
Temple of Hephaistos
(The Thesefon),
Athens, *c.* 449 B.C.

2. GREEK IONIC.
The Erechtheion,
Athens, *c.* 421 B.C.

3. GREEK CORINTHIAN.
Monument of Lysicrates,
Athens, *c.* 334 B.C.

4. GREEK DORIC IN ITALY.
Temple of Demeter,
Paestum, *c.* 510 B.C.

5. ROMAN DORIC.
Theatre of Marcellus,
Rome, 23–13 B.C.

6. ROMAN IONIC.
Temple of Fortuna
Virilis,
Rome, 100–40 B.C.

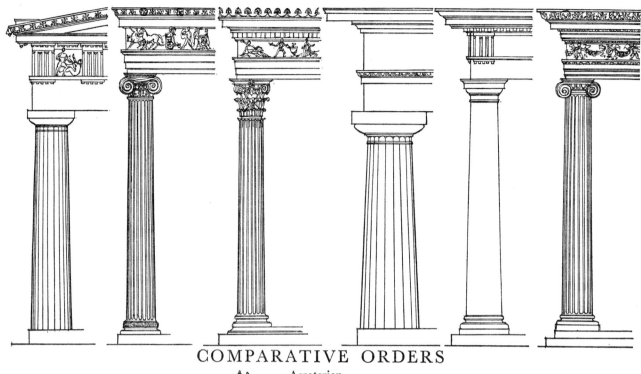

COMPARATIVE ORDERS

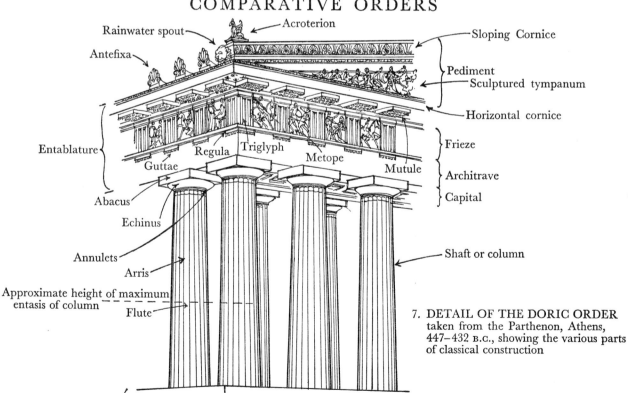

Rainwater spout — Acroterion — Sloping Cornice

Antefixa

Pediment
Sculptured tympanum

Horizontal cornice

Entablature

Regula · Triglyph · Frieze

Guttae · Metope · Mutule · Architrave

Abacus · Capital

Echinus

Annulets · Shaft or column

Arris

Approximate height of maximum
entasis of column

Flute

7. DETAIL OF THE DORIC ORDER
taken from the Parthenon, Athens,
447–432 B.C., showing the various parts
of classical construction

Stylobate

8

THE ORDERS, CONSTRUCTION AND ORNAMENT

8. ROMAN CORINTHIAN.
The Pantheon,
Rome, A.D. 120

9. ROMAN COMPOSITE.
Arch of Titus,
Rome, A.D. 81

10. ITALIAN BAROQUE.
Doric/Tuscan.
S. Peter's Piazza, Rome,
Bernini, 1656–67

11. ITALIAN RENAISSANCE
DORIC.
S. Pietro in Montorio, Rome,
Bramante, 1500

12. ITALIAN
RENAISSANCE
CORINTHIAN.
Il Gesù, Rome,
Della Porta, 1573

13. ITALIAN BAROQUE
COMPOSITE.
S. Agnese, Rome,
Borromini, 1645

COMPARATIVE ORDERS

Greek moulding ornament

15. Egg and dart

16. Leaf and dart

17. Bead and reel

14. Doorway detail,
the Erechtheion, Athens

19. Anthemion (honeysuckle)
decoration

18. Doric capital, Temple
of Poseidon, Paestum

20. Corinthian capital, Monument
of Lysicrates, Athens

23. Ionic capital, the
Erechtheion, Athens

21. The Greek acanthus (spinosus) leaf

22. The Roman acanthus
(mollis) leaf

9

covered (apart from the mainland and islands) the Greek colonies in Italy, Sicily and Asia Minor. The remains in Italy and Sicily are of the earlier period, almost archaic, and it is interesting to compare them with the perfection of the style to be seen in mid-5th century Athens. The Greeks built in marble where possible. This was plentiful in Greece and lent itself to accurate fitting of blocks, detailed carving and crisp lining of flutes and arrises. Where the usual building material was stone, as in southern Italy, they made a stucco paste of powdered marble and coated the stone to provide a layer suitable for fine carving. This stucco veneer has, of course, now largely weathered away and the temples at Paestum in Italy, for instance, do not glisten in the sun as does the Parthenon in Athens. *Temples* were important buildings and their remains provide us with information about design and construction. A typical plan (25) shows a building erected on a stylobate three steps high. The rectangular temple is then formed by an exterior colonnade which supports an entablature and end pediments which acted as gables to carry a low-pitched roof. The roofs were of timber covered by marble or terracotta tiling. Inside the colonnade was a walled room (the *naos*), which might also have a colonnade, and which generally contained the shrine of the deity with an adjoining room for the treasury. People did not worship in the temple, as in a church, but outside it. Fig. 7, taken from the Parthenon, shows the named parts of temple construction.

Greek *town planning* was evolved on the gridiron pattern and the chief early example of this was Piraeus, port of Athens, laid out by Hippodamus of Miletus in the mid-5th century. In this type of plan, streets are wide and cross one another at right angles. The centre of a Greek city, particularly in earlier days, was, for safety's sake, built on a hill which was ringed by walled fortifications. Such a hill city was called an *acropolis* – a literal translation

– and that in Athens, where stand the most magnificent of the 5th century Greek temples, is the most famous.

In the process of evolving a standard of perfection in proportion and form of their trabeated architecture the Greeks created the *system of orders*. They had three: *Doric*, *Ionic* and *Corinthian*. Each order had its own individual proportions for each part, its own form of ornament and permitted mouldings and a rigid set of rules was established for the proportion of each part in relationship to the others. Thus, though buildings might vary in size, the individual parts of the order were adjusted accordingly and remained in proportion with one another. The Greeks never used a part of one order with a part of another and rarely employed more than one order on the façade of a building though there might be one used on the exterior and another inside. Later exponents of classical forms did both these things.

Each order consists (1–6, 8–13) of a vertical *column* or support, a *base* below (not always used) and a *capital* above. On the capital is carried the horizontal member called the *entablature* which, in turn, is sub-divided into three parts: the lowest member is the *architrave*, either plain or divided into fasciae, the next is the *frieze*, plain or sculptured and above is the projecting set of mouldings comprising the *cornice* which contains the draining waterspouts (often in the form of lions' heads) and is decorated along the top edge by antefixae. If a triangular *pediment* is used, as in temple design, the cornice moulding is continued along the top of the pediment forming a sloping and a horizontal cornice (7). The triangular space in the pediment is called the *tympanum* and is often sculptured. It is the famous sculpture from the Parthenon pediments as well as the interior frieze which comprise the 'Elgin Marbles' in the British Museum.

The Greeks preferred the *Doric Order* as can be

seen in the best examples in Greece (1, 7). The proportions and refinements reached their highest peak of perfection in the mid-5th century. There is no base. The column stands on a three-step stylobate and has a fluted shaft. The number of flutes per column varies but in the Parthenon (accepted as the superb masterpiece) there are 20 shallow flutes rising to sharp arrises between (7). The Doric capital consists of a square block (the *abacus*) and below this a subtly curved *echinus* and annular rings cut into the column. The entablature, generally one quarter the height of the order, has a plain architrave and a strongly projecting cornice under whose soffit are flat blocks called *mutules* which have 18 *guttae* in three rows of six beneath. The frieze of the Doric Order is distinctive: it is divided into *triglyphs* and *metopes*. The triglyphs are placed one over each column and one between and have vertical channels carved in them. Between are the square metopes, generally sculptured. At the corners the arrangement differs in sophisticated designs like the Parthenon to present a triglyph at the corner itself though, in archaic models, this is not always so. The frieze is separated from the architrave by the regula moulding; there are six guttae beneath each triglyph.

The *Ionic Order* has a narrower, slender shaft and a moulded base. The flutes are semi-circular not shallow, generally 24 in number and are separated by fillets not sharp arrises (2). Its capital is distinguished by two scrolled volutes at the sides, while between, the echinus is carved in egg and dart decoration and the necking below in anthemion (23). The entablature is one fifth of the order and has a triple fascia architrave, a plain or continuously sculptured frieze and a cornice less strongly projecting than the Doric, without mutules. The *Corinthian Order* was not often used by the Greeks. It is very similar to the Ionic in entablature, column and base but has a different capital (3, 20). This distinctive and beautiful capital has a four-faced abacus. Below this it is shaped like a concave bell and is decorated by two rows of acanthus leaves rising to corner volutes or has a lower row of palm leaves with acanthus above (20). The *best examples* in *Greece* of these orders are Doric: the *Theseion* and the *Parthenon*, Athens (1, 7); Ionic: the *Erechtheion*, Athens (2, 23); and Corinthian: the *Monument of Lysicrates*, Athens (3, 20).

Greek remains in *Italy* are in the southern part of the peninsular, primarily at Paestum (called Poseidonia by the Greeks) and in Sicily. These are all Doric temples and are all of a fairly early period representing the early proportions of the order. The entablature mouldings are simple, the abacus is very large, the echinus also and not in a sophisticated curve, while the columns are short, vigorously strong and wide and have a pronounced *entasis*.* At *Paestum* there are three temples of which two are large and well-preserved. The *Temple of Poseidon* (Hera) dates from 460 B.C. and is one of the very few Greek temples extant which still possesses some of its upper row of columns which supported the roof. Most large temples had such upper columns but these have disappeared (18, 27). The *Temple of Demeter*, nearby, is also large and exceptionally well-preserved (24). These temples are of travertine stone and were originally coated with marble stucco and decoratively carved. In *Sicily* there are a

* Taken from the Greek word for distension, an entasis is an outward curving along the outline of a column shaft (7). This is one of a number of different means used by the Greeks to correct the optical illusions created in looking at horizontal and vertical straight lines which tend to appear to be concave. In the Parthenon, for example, all such lines and planes are curved—stylobate, cornice, entablature, pediment, columns. There are no true vertical or horizontal surface planes or lines in the temple: all planes are curved convexly, but the curves are so subtly worked out that they appear to be flat planes. In more archaic work, as at Paestum, the curves are obvious.

24. Temple of Demeter (Athena). Paestum, Italy, c. 510 B.C.

25. General plan of temple lay-out in Italy and Sicily

NAOS PRO NAOS

26. Temple of Concord, Agrigento, Sicily, 5th century B.C.

27. Temple of Poseidon (Hera), Paestum, c. 460 B.C. Interior showing upper row of columns

28. Theatre at Syracuse, Sicily, 3rd to 2nd century B.C.

number of Greek centres: *Agrigento, Selinunte, Segesta* and *Syracuse*. At Agrigento, on the south coast of the island, is the well-preserved *Temple of Concord* (26) which was later converted into a church. At Syracuse, the Baroque cathedral incorporates the original Greek *temple of Athena* and, inside the cathedral, one can still see twelve of the 28-foot-high Doric columns set into the aisles, still standing on their original stylobate. At Syracuse also there remain fragments of the town laid out in the 4th century B.C. and the Greek *theatre* there which dates from the 3rd century (28). Like most other Greek theatres, the orchestra was reduced to a semi-circle in Roman times. The original Greek pattern is shown in the plan in Fig. 29 which is taken from the restored theatre at Epidauros in the Peloponnese.

Greek *ornament*, like the architecture and the orders, provides the foundation for all classical design. It was of the highest quality and has never been surpassed. Decoration was used sparingly and always to enhance, not obscure, the architectural form. Sculpture also was an integral part of the building design, generally applied to pediments and friezes. Each moulding was assigned its allotted ornament in Greek work and all the forms were simple, delicate and exquisitely carved. The most common motifs are the acanthus leaf* (3, 8, 9, 12, 13, 20), the anthemion or honeysuckle (14, 19, 23), the egg and dart (or life and death) (15), the leaf and dart (16), the bead and reel (17), the guilloche which resembles a triple plait, the dentil (3, 5, 10) and the scroll. All these were repeated all through the dominant periods of classical architecture but never as superbly as in Athenian Greek work of the 5th century B.C.

* The acanthus *spinosus* leaf was used in Greek ornament. This is a spikier variety (21) than the Roman acanthus *mollis* which has more rounded tips to the leaves (22).

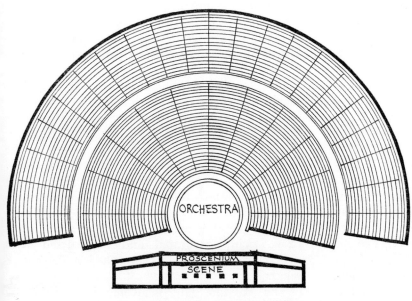

29. Sketch plan of Greek theatre (Epidauros)

Other notable buildings of the period

Agrigento, Sicily:
    Temple of Hera, *c.* 470 B.C.
    Temple of Zeus Olympius, *c.* 470 B.C.
Segesta, Sicily: Temple, *c.* 430 B.C.
Selinunte, Sicily: Temples, especially
    Temple of Apollo, *c.* 540 B.C.

CHAPTER 2

Roman 146 B.C. to A.D. 476

WHILE the Hellenic culture in Ancient Greece was preceded by the Minoan and Mycenaean civilisations which were not without influence upon the later, purer Greek work, a similar relationship was held by the Etruscans in respect of later Ancient Rome. Archaeological research is still providing knowledge about the Etruscan peoples and their culture and, though remains are not extensive and the language is still not understood, it is now realised that these peoples, who inhabited central Italy from the 8th to the 1st century B.C., had a high standard of building, literary and visual arts, lived in cities and practised methods of construction in advance of their time including the arch, the vault and the decorative use of terracotta and metals. 19th century historians gave credit to Ancient Rome for a number of these developments, now recognised to be of Etruscan origin.

It is generally accepted that the Etruscan peoples migrated to Italy from further east–Asia Minor, Greece, the Orient possibly–and settled in the area between the rivers Arno and Tiber. They were great builders and used large stones (often without cement) and frequently in polygonal block form. They created arches with radiating voussoirs and used the extension of this principle to produce barrel vaulting with dressed stones. Controversy over the origins of this true arch construction– whether Etruscan or Roman–continues because extant Etruscan examples date from the 3rd century B.C. onwards and the Romans conquered the Etruscan civilisation about 280 B.C. Among existing arches of this type is the *town gateway* at *Volterra* (near Siena) (30), the *Arch of Augustus* at *Perugia* (35) with the *Porta Marzia* nearby and an earlier example, the *Porta Sanguinaria* at *Ferentino*. A much earlier

type, of simple lintel design, is the 6th century *Porta Saracena* now on the mountainous outskirts of the town of *Segni*. It is in *Rome* that the most famous example still exists. This is the *Cloaca Maxima*, built as a flood water drain by the Etruscans in the 6th century B.C. to drain the later Forum Romanum. For many years this was thought to be the earliest example of the true arch in Europe but it is now recognised that, though the drain dates from the 6th century, it was roofed over with its present three concentric rings of radiating voussoirs in 184 B.C. For those who wish to discover its whereabouts (it is rarely mentioned in guide books) it can still be seen at its exit into the Tiber from the Ponte Rotto near the east bank.

Only small parts of *Etruscan temples* exist but an interesting example from *Alatri* has been set up in the gardens of the Etruscan Museum in Rome, the *Villa Giulia* (34). On the temple and in the museum are excellent sections of Etruscan terracotta decoration showing its characteristic form (31, 32) using scrolls, key designs and the anthemion or honeysuckle pattern. (Compare with the Greek examples in Chapter 1.) Many *Etruscan tombs* exist, both of the type dug into the earth and known for their decoration by fresco painting as at *Tarquinia* and in the tumulus mounds of the sort to be found at *Cerveteri*. A proto-Ionic capital is illustrated in Fig. 33 from one of the tombs there. Such tombs contain reconstructions of houses and display personal belongings and domestic utensils; they are, in some cases, richly decorated and constructed with coffered ceilings or beams supported on decorative pillars.

The Palatine Hill in Rome is traditionally accepted as the site of the origins of Ancient Rome,

30. Town Gateway, Volterra, 3rd century B.C.

31 and 32. Details from 34

33. Capital from tomb at Cerveteri, 5th century B.C.

34. Temple from Alatri (now in gardens of Villa Giulia, Rome)

35. Arch of Augustus, Perugia, 3rd century B.C.

where a tribe of people settled and established their city. From a tribe they extended by the 5th century into a republic which expanded over all Italy and in 146 B.C. took over Ancient Greece. This was, however, not the end of Roman ambition but the beginning. Domination extended to North Africa, Egypt and over much of known Europe. The republic became an empire in 27 B.C. which grew larger, stronger, more powerful as time passed.

Architecturally the great creations of Rome were under the empire not the republic and the best work was produced between the Age of Augustus, the first emperor, and the 3rd century A.D. After this deterioration and decline set in aesthetically as well as economically and militarily. The building history of Ancient Rome is a lengthy one, probably longer than that of any other European empire, and of complex nature. This complexity shows most clearly the fundamental and numerous differences between the classical architecture of Greece as described in chapter one and that of Rome. One of these is not inferior or superior to the other, though individual taste may incline one's preference in either direction. The achievements of both civilisations were supreme (at their best) but in different fields. To sum up such differences in the simplest terms would be to describe the Greek approach as artistic, essentially simple and engaged in a search for perfection on limited grounds while the Roman achievement is in impressive, large-scale creations, fundamentally sound in construction, varied in concept, rich in decoration and colour, exploiting the full engineering possibilities of media and architectural form. To illustrate: the supreme Greek achievement was the Parthenon, with mathematical and aesthetic perfection of the trabeated architectural medium (7), while Roman greatness is typified by the great vaults and decorative interiors of the Roman Baths, their road and bridge system,* the many aqueducts which supplied water for baths and fountains to a capital city based on the dry Campagna, the Pantheon (61–4) with its vast dome and the Colosseum (43) incorporating the best of Greek and Roman constructional ideas.

Extensive building schemes under the Empire

* Typical of Roman quality of construction in this field are bridges (36). That at *Rimini* still bears the modern traffic of the busy Via Flaminia over its metal plate surface (38) and the oldest bridge in *Rome* over the Tiber is also still in use (37). Almost all such bridges are in stone with a level roadway.

36. Ponte dei Cappuccini Ascoli Piceno.
River Tronto

37. Ponte Fabrizio (Pons Fabricius) Rome, 61–21 B.C. Spans half of River Tiber to the Isola Tiberina in centre of river

and under specific Roman Emperors–Augustus, Tiberius, Titus, Hadrian, Septimius Severus, Caracalla, Diocletian–were projected in Rome, in Italy and all over the Empire. Wherever Roman civilisation went so were created *cities*, each with their buildings necessary to Roman life. As with the Greeks, the ideal *Roman town plan* was on gridiron pattern but where the town existed already adaptations were made. The city was always encircled by defensive walls with town gates at intervals. The roads within this area crossed one another at right angles and, where later Medieval planning has not obscured this, the pattern can still be seen. An eight-sided city was considered the ideal layout for such a plan. *Vitruvius* (Marcus Vitruvius Pollio) the discovery of whose manuscripts '*de Architectura*' provided the basis for much of the Italian Renaissance designs and the later English work of Inigo Jones and the Palladian School, set out his plans in the 1st century B.C. for such cities.

The centre of Roman city life was the *forum*. This corresponded to the Greek agora. Under the Republic, the Roman forum was such a market place surrounded by shops; under the Empire it tended to be more a centre for large important buildings– temples, basilicas, baths–though still a public meeting place. Large towns had more than one forum as, for example, *Rome*, which acquired a new one under each important emperor. The *Forum Romanum* is the chief one in Rome, now fully excavated and, due to the silting up of the site by subsequent building, is now some feet below the level of the modern street alongside it. In the Middle Ages it was grazing land for cattle, hence its name 'Campo Vaccino', and the greatest damage to its buildings was done, not by the barbarians who sacked the city in the 5th century, but by its use as a marble quarry for Medieval building. The nearby Colosseum and Basilica of Constantine were other sufferers. Such depradations were, to some extent, excusable in an age which did not recognise any value in classical architecture, but they continued long afterwards. One 17th century example gave rise to the saying '*Quod non fecerunt barbari, fecerunt Barberini*'. This refers to the despoiling of the Pantheon which had survived in remarkable condition from barbarian raids, but which lost the bronze of its portico roof when the Barberini Pope Urban VIII took it away to erect other buildings.

Two famous *triumphal arches* remain in the Forum

38. Bridge of Tiberius (Augustus), Rimini. The Via Flaminia over River Marecchia, A.D. 14–20

B

Romanum, that of *Septimius Severus*, A.D. 204, at one end of the *Via Sacra* and that of *Titus*, A.D. 81, one of the earliest, at the other end. The Arch of Titus (40, 48) is generally regarded as the finest example extant of the single-arched type and the Composite Order was used here* for the first time. The design is dignified, well-proportioned and has restrained decoration. Especially interesting are the sculptured panels inside the arch commemorating the Capture of Jerusalem in A.D. 70. One of the ruins in the Forum here which inspired many Renaissance and Baroque architects in Italy, Michelangelo for instance, is the *Basilica of Constantine* (Maxentius) also along the *Via Sacra*. Begun in A.D. 308, it was one of the most imposing structures of Ancient Rome, with massive concrete piers, 14 feet in diameter, supporting an enormous vaulted roof of which some of the empty coffers are still visible. In front of these piers stood a row of gigantic marble columns one of which was taken away by Pope Paul V and set in front of the Church of S. Maria Maggiore in the city.

Roman variety in building form was partly made possible by a wide range of *materials*. The Greeks had used marble predominantly. The Romans also used stone of many varieties and brick which they faced with marble. Their chief contribution in this field was concrete which they employed widely, in combination with brick, as a basic constructional material. The strength and durability of Roman concrete was tremendous due to their use of the substance *pozzolana*: a volcanic ash found near Naples and named after a nearby village. Mixed with lime from the local stone it formed an exceedingly hard concrete to which base were added fragments of brick and travertine. This provided a solid core for walling and vaulting and made possible the construction of the vast vaults in the

baths and basilicas which, a thousand years later, inspired Renaissance architects to build their church cupolas. The dome of the Pantheon, for instance, was never surpassed in size in Renaissance or Baroque Italy even by the Basilica of S. Peter in Rome. Roman concrete was poured between boards to build walls and over centering for arches and vaults. Marble was not in general use in Rome until after the 1st century B.C. This gives substance to the boast of Augustus Caesar that when he came to Rome it was a city of bricks and he left it a city of marble. It was in his time (27 B.C.) that the marble quarries at Carrara were developed and further Greek white marble imported from Hymettos and Pentelicus. By the 1st and 2nd century A.D. marble was being brought to Rome from all over the Empire to be used mainly for facings to vaults, walls and floors. Because of the quantity available of such beautifully grained coloured marbles Roman columns were often unfluted and monolithic (in contrast to Greek white marble ones). Despite this quantity of marble left in Ancient Rome in the 5th century A.D. on all the great buildings, little remains today due to its removal for later building purposes. On less costly buildings, marble stucco was used as a facing to brick and concrete structures. Thinner coats of such stucco were added to decorative surfaces.

Constructionally *Roman classical architecture* was more broadly based than the Greek. Whereas the Greeks had adhered to the trabeated form and had developed it to the ultimate perfection, the Romans, whose building needs were far more diversified, used the arcuated form also. They did not abandon trabeated building but tended to keep the orders as decorative features and constructed the building on arcuated principles. They used the semi-circular arch, enriched and moulded and, from this, evolved barrel and intersecting vaults. Many Roman buildings show both forms of construction together. Two particular examples in

* Triumphal arches and town gateways were elaborate and varied and many fine examples still exist. Three other Italian arches are shown in 39, 41, 42.

TRIUMPHAL ARCHES AND TOWN GATEWAYS

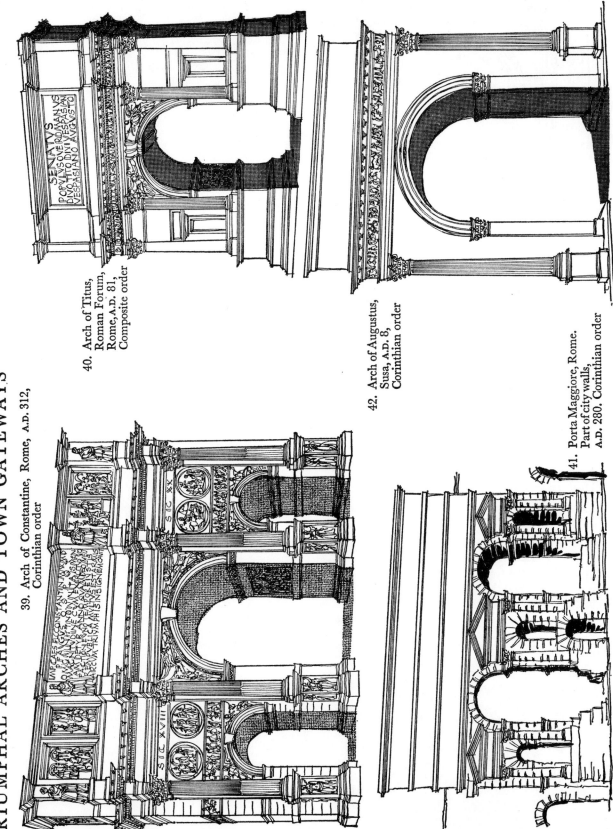

39. Arch of Constantine, Rome, A.D. 312,
Corinthian order

40. Arch of Titus,
Roman Forum,
Rome, A.D. 81,
Composite order

42. Arch of Augustus,
Susa, A.D. 8,
Corinthian order

41. Porta Maggiore, Rome.
Part of city walls,
A.D. 280. Corinthian order

44. The Colosseum, third storey detail (Corinthian)

43. Colosseum, Rome, A.D. 70–82

45. Verona interior showing arena and auditorium c. A.D. 300

Rome are the *Colosseum* and the *Theatre of Marcellus* (43, 47). Comparing these two designs with the Greek temples in 7, 24 and 26, an entirely different architectural form emerges, though still using the classical formula. The *Colosseum* illustrates the classic instance of the Roman use of orders, one per storey, with Doric Order at the bottom and above, in order of ascent, Ionic, Corinthian (44) and Corinthian (the top storey being in pilaster not three-quarter column form). The columns are all lined up one above the other on the amphitheatre façade and the entablatures act as string courses. Since the basic construction is arcuated the proportions of the orders (which are not load-bearing) can be altered; liberties are taken here which were never undertaken in Greece. The Colosseum is, even in ruin, a magnificent erection, aesthetically and constructionally. The interior has been despoliated for later building purposes but the façade is still a fine silhouette. Built of travertine blocks, held together by metal cramps but without mortar, it is 157 feet high and has an elliptical section with major and minor axes of 620 and 513 feet respectively; it is the largest amphitheatre in the world. It was built to accommodate 50,000 people.

The exterior façades of most Roman theatres and amphitheatres followed this pattern of construction. Still in use for open air performances of opera is the *amphitheatre* at *Verona*, A.D. 290. In contrast to the Colosseum, the exterior is badly damaged but the interior is almost complete (45). *Roman theatres*, unlike Greek ones which were built into the hillside, were generally free-standing. A classic example, though now in poor condition, is the *Theatre of Marcellus* in *Rome*, near the Capitol Hill (5, 47). Only two tiers of the wall arcade survive, with the Doric Order below and Ionic above. The proportion and detail are still of high standard and illustrate well the combination of arcuated and trabeated construction. The Romans utilised Greek theatres all over the Empire, adapting the circular orchestras to their own part circle plan. That at *Taormina* in Sicily (46) and those in the ancient cities of *Ostia* and *Pompeii* are examples (70).

The construction of the barrel and intersecting *vault* was an important Roman contribution to architectural development. Due to their use of the inert concrete material the Romans were able to build vast spans, providing a rigid covering to large spaces and, as in the great thermal baths, avoiding columnar support in the large central spaces. Some vaults were made with brick ribs and concrete infilling while in the later days of the Empire some stone vaults were built. The Romans constructed few domes–this architectural form was exploited in Byzantine work. Roman decoration to vaulted ceilings was often by coffering. These coffers were sunken panels in circular, octagonal or square form, moulded and carved (52). Paint, gilt and marble veneer were used as decorative covering.

The Romans continued to use the *system of orders* initiated by the Greeks but evolved five types from the original three. The *Roman Doric Order* is less refined and less solid than the Greek. It is often unfluted and, being slenderer, needs a base. The capital is less subtly drawn as can be seen in the echinus moulding which has a semi-circular section instead of the Greek curve (5, 47, 67, 74). Provincial examples are sometimes coarser as in the Forum colonnade at Pompeii where the entasis is crudely obvious (73). An alternative version is presented by the *Roman Tuscan Order* which is unfluted and very plain. Roman examples have vanished but Renaissance architects revived it from drawings in Vitruvius' '*de Architectura*'. Bernini used it in the piazza colonnade of S. Peter's in Rome (10).

Roman Ionic is very similar to the Greek. The mouldings have more enrichment and sometimes the corner volutes are turned to face both elevations (6, 47, 54, 68, 73). The *Corinthian Order* was very popular with Roman architects; its richness of carving and the similarity of all four faces of the

ROMAN THEATRES

46. Taormina, Sicily. Originally Greek, adapted to Roman designs

47. Theatre of Marcellus, Rome, 23–13 B.C. At present in ruinous state. This drawing shows a restored theatre. Upper storeys above Doric and Ionic colonnades do not exist in this form now

capital made it suitable for their buildings and arches. The acanthus decoration is different and softer than the Greek (21, 22) and the order ornately decorated (8, 39, 42, 44, 49, 50, 57–9, 62, 64–5). The *Composite Order*, invented by the Romans, is, as its name suggests, a combination of two other orders. It takes its large corner volutes from the Ionic design and the bell-shaped, acanthus-leafed capital, also the entablature, from the Corinthian. The upper row of Corinthian acanthus leaves is replaced in the Composite Order by an echinus moulding carved in egg and tongue ornament above and bead and reel underneath. It became the favourite Roman order especially for triumphal arches (9, 40, 48).

Roman ornament is also taken from the Greek form with the same enrichment of mouldings and same designs in anthemion, acanthus, fret and guilloche patterns. Roman interpretation of these forms was freer and sometimes coarser. The Romans also used a greater quantity of ornament, covering a greater surface area in relationship to the plain field so that, in some cases, the effect is self-destructive. They used scroll decoration with acanthus in arabesques and intertwined in this birds, animals, children, cherub heads and mythical creatures such as griffins. Interiors were colourful, faced in marble veneer or had painted designs and gilded and painted sculpture in relief or in the round (22, 51, 53, 60, 72).

Typically Roman was the *basilica*: the hall of justice and centre for commercial exchange. Ironically it was the basilica which was later used as the foundation for Early Christian church design (not the religious temple) and this form has persisted to the present day. The Roman basilica was rectangular, about twice as long as wide and had a semi-circular apse at each end. Earlier designs had timber roofs supported on a row of columns on each side of the central passage (later the church nave) and had narrower side aisles with lower roofs. Later, larger examples had concrete vaulting carried on large concrete and brick piers. Typical of the latter type was the *Basilica of Constantine* (already referred to, page 18). The *Basilica of Trajan*, A.D. 98–112, in Rome was of timber roof type and this was carried on 96 granite columns. Only fragments exist of this in the Trajan Forum.

In contrast, the *Roman temple* owes much of its plan and design to the Greek prototype. It was in temple architecture that the Romans retained trabeated construction though they did not orientate the temple as the Greeks did, so that the rising sun would light up the statue, but towards the forum. The Roman cella (naos) was larger than the Greek in order to house treasure and it encroached on the peristyle. Sometimes this was so cramped that the colonnade was set as half-columns into the wall of the cella, lining up with the columns of the portico which stood free at the entrance front. Many Roman temples were built on a podium instead of the Greek stylobate and were approached up a flight of steps (55). Most examples were in the Corinthian Order or the Ionic but rarely (in contrast to the Greek) Doric. One of the best remaining temples in Italy is that of *Fortuna Virilis* in Rome near the Tiber (6, 54). In the *Forum Romanum* are a number of which *Antoninus and Faustina*, A.D. 142 (60) (now the Church of S. Lorenzo) and *Romulus* (57) (now the Church of S.S. Cosmo and Damiano) are in fair condition, while dramatic fragments remain of *Castor and Pollux*, A.D. 6, *Vespasian*, A.D. 94, *Concord* and *Saturn*.

Circular temples possess a round cella and an encircling colonnade (56). Fragments remain of the *Temple of Vesta* in the *Forum Romanum*, A.D. 205, though much more complete is the other *Temple of Vesta* in the *Forum Boarium* near Fortuna Virilis. This has its Corinthian peristyle of 20 marble columns almost intact but the entablature has been replaced by a roof. The temple dates from about

23

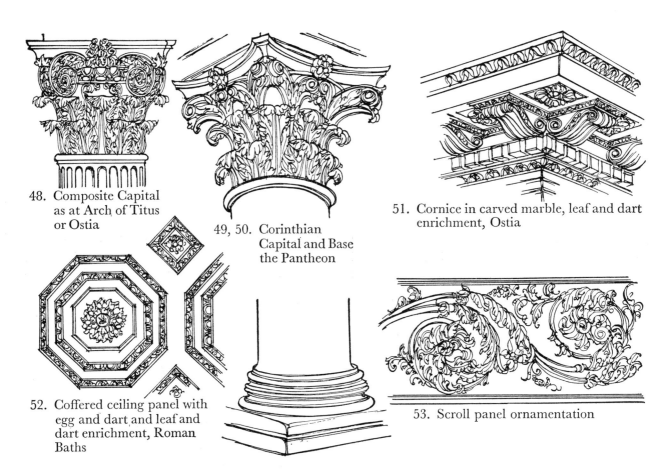

48. Composite Capital as at Arch of Titus or Ostia

49, 50. Corinthian Capital and Base the Pantheon

51. Cornice in carved marble, leaf and dart enrichment, Ostia

52. Coffered ceiling panel with egg and dart and leaf and dart enrichment, Roman Baths

53. Scroll panel ornamentation

30 B.C. and is very Greek in its detail and proportion (58, 59). The most famous of all Roman circular temples is the *Pantheon* in Rome which has been in continuous use first as a temple then as a church since it was built in A.D. 120.* The building consists of a circular cella and a 16 columned portico (61). The portico is in the Corinthian Order with monolithic granite columns and white Pentelic marble capitals and bases supporting an entablature and pediment (64). Inside is a finely proportioned doorway, 40 feet high with 26-feet-high bronze doors. These ancient doors were originally gold plated. The Pantheon interior is more impressive and is so well proportioned that its vast size is not immediately apparent (62). There are no windows and the only lighting, adequate and impressive, is from the unglazed oculus in the centre of the top of the dome. It is 30 feet across and 142 feet above the floor. The construction of the concrete dome was an incredible feat of engineering and has not been surpassed. It has a diameter of 142 feet and is coffered in five concentric rings. It diminishes in thickness from about 40 feet at the springing to 5

* The inscription on the frieze of the portico relating to Agrippa who built a temple on the site in 27 B.C. was replaced by Hadrian when he built his Pantheon in A.D. 120.

feet at the top and was built up in horizontal layers of brick and concrete. The cement was poured onto the hemispherical centering into which the coffered panels had been set.

The dome is carried on eight massive piers and relieving arches are set into the walls to reinforce the latter and concentrate the load on the piers. The order is Corinthian, the decoration in marble, including the floor, and the whole is of one design, form and scheme. The Pantheon has survived varied reigns and cultures. It was re-dedicated from its original purpose (a temple to all the gods) as a Christian Church, the Madonna and All Martyrs, in A.D. 609.

The great *thermal establishments* were a vital part of Roman life. Living conditions at home for many lacked space and comfort and the public baths provided cheaply the means for daily bathing, relaxation and refreshment to partake of sport, entertainment, receive medical attention or to converse or carry out business as desired. These baths varied in size and scope but no town was without one or more; in Imperial Rome there were over 800. The larger ones had lecture theatres, concert halls, sports stadia, restaurants, theatres, gardens and fountains. The baths themselves

ROMAN TEMPLES

54. Temple of Fortuna Virilis, Forum Boarium, Rome, 100–40 B.C

CELLA

55, 56. Typical temple plans

57. Temple of Romulus (now church of SS. Cosmo and Damiano) Forum Romanum, Rome. Original bronze doors, A.D. 307

58. Temple of Vesta, Forum Boarium, Rome, 30–10 B.C.

59. Capital, Temple of Vesta

60. Entablature, Temple of Antoninus and Faustina, Rome, A.D. 160

provided hot and cool rooms with swimming pools. Heating was by hypocaust wherein hot air was passed through hollow bricks in the walls and floors from furnaces underneath. The temperature could be varied accurately. The great thermae of Rome were vast buildings of which only ruins exist but even these have inspired architects of the Renaissance and later to build Roman Imperial style interiors with enormous halls supporting vaulted roofs on marble columns. The two most famous examples in Rome were the *Baths of Caracalla* (now used for open air opera performances) and the *Baths of Diocletian*. The Caracalla Thermae, built A.D. 206–17, covered an area larger than that of the Palace of Westminster in London, the main building block alone encompassing 270,000 square feet. The Baths of Diocletian were larger still (A.D. 284–304) and accommodated 3200 bathers. An interesting feature is that the tepidarium was converted in A.D. 1563 by Michelangelo into the nave of the Church of S. Maria degli Angeli and the architect retained the circular domed caldarium as an entrance vestibule. Although the building is now decorated internally in Renaissance style with ecclesiastical fittings, the original vault survives.

Domestic architecture, whether palaces, villas, houses, flats or whole towns present some of the most interesting remains. The great *palaces* on the *Palatine Hill* in *Rome* overlooking the Forum exist in only fragmentary condition. On this beautiful site, over several centuries, the Roman Emperors created their imperial residences, richly decorated and elaborately constructed. Most magnificent was Nero's 'Golden House' which covered an immense area and included a lake where the Colosseum now stands. Of greater interest for its extensive remains is *Hadrian's Villa* near *Tivoli* which he built over several square miles of terraced hillside (65–9). Villa is a misnomer for it included several thermae, stadia, halls, theatres, magnificent gardens, terraces and fountains as well as the imperial apartments. Hadrian was an outstanding architect himself and here he gave vent to one of his interests. Most of the marble and treasures have gone–destroyed, re-used or now in museums–but a clearer idea can be gained here than elsewhere of what such Roman palaces were like. Especially interesting is the layout known as 'Canopus' (65, 66). Hadrian based this on the Temple of Serapis and the Canal of Canopus in the city of that name near Alexandria where the cult of the god Serapis flourished. In his villa the Serapeum is a vast semicircular hall covered with a half-dome originally worked in white mosaic. Much of the sculpture found on the site has now been put *in situ* by the archaeologists.

The three cities of *Pompeii, Herculaneum* and *Ostia* provide fascinating material for those who wish to study Roman town planning, houses, shops, fora, baths, etc. At Pompeii and Herculaneum the towns have been remarkably preserved over the centuries by their covering of lava and ash. *Pompeii* was an irregularly planned provincial city of 20,000 inhabitants. Of especial interest are the streets with their pedestrian crossings and drinking fountains (71), the forum (73), which is fairly complete with temples and basilica, and the theatres, baths and houses. There are two theatres and an amphitheatre (70) and three sets of baths. The Forum Baths are remarkably complete, with fine stucco and terracotta decoration (72). The houses are unique in the preservation of Roman town domestic architecture, showing the 1st century A.D. type of design. The street façade is narrow with shop fronts and the houses extend back to include the peristyle with gardens and fountains (74). They were private, spacious, suitable for the climate and beautifully decorated with wall paintings, mosaic and sculpture.

Ostia is less well known than Pompeii but is just as interesting. It was occupied over a longer period

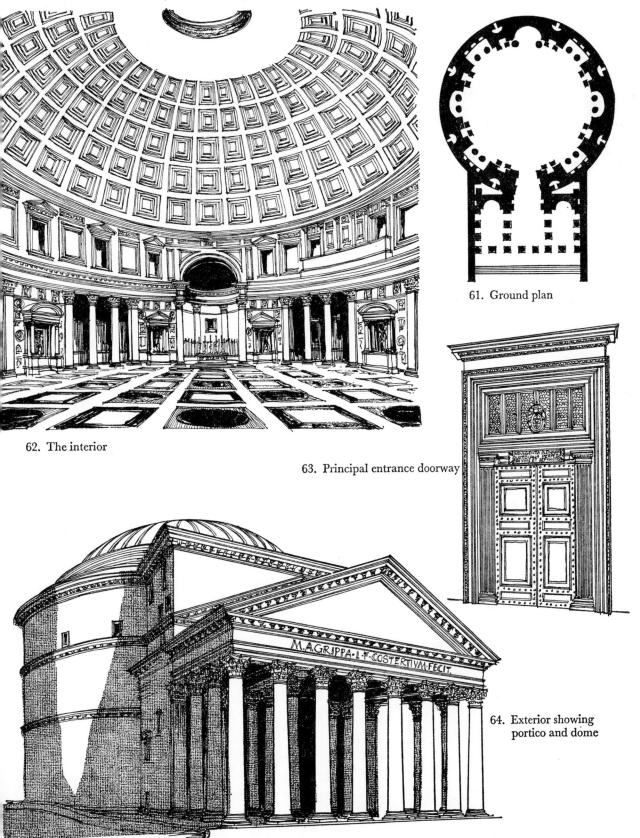

62. The interior

61. Ground plan

63. Principal entrance doorway

64. Exterior showing portico and dome

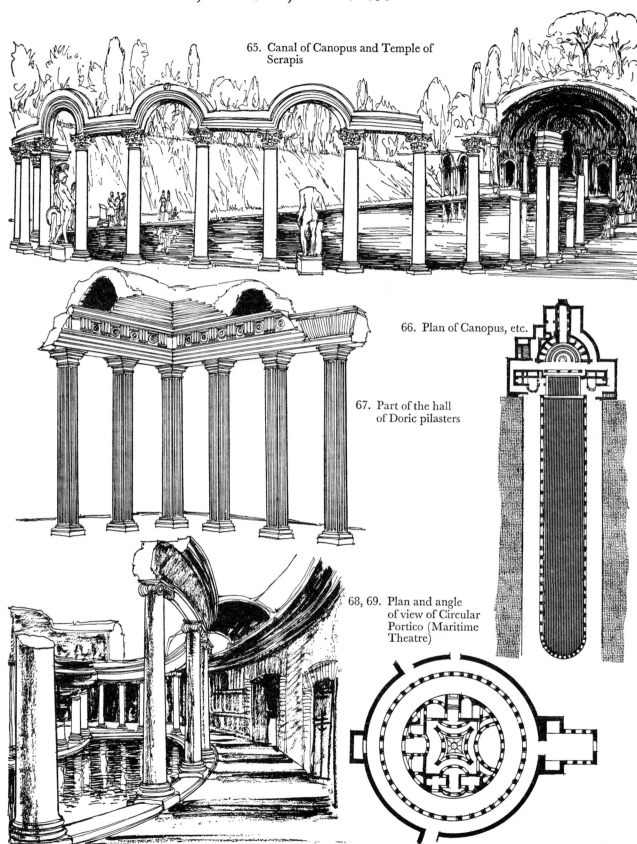

65. Canal of Canopus and Temple of Serapis

66. Plan of Canopus, etc.

67. Part of the hall of Doric pilasters

68, 69. Plan and angle of view of Circular Portico (Maritime Theatre)

(4th century B.C. to 3rd century A.D.) and was not a provincial town but the port of Rome and thus much larger and more important. The Tiber changed its course in 1557 and Ostia Antica (as it is now called) is not now by the sea. As at Pompeii, there are streets, squares, baths, theatre, temples and basilicas (48, 51). The Baths of Neptune possess fine floor mosaics and those at the Forum have a well preserved frigidarium and a complete example of public toilets with 20 marble seats and washing facilities. But, like Pompeii, the most unusual feature is the preservation of domestic architecture and, here, less in houses but in blocks of flats, more suited to a busy port than individual houses. Such blocks of flats must also have existed in Rome. The Ostia examples had three or four storeys and were up to 50 feet high. They had shops on the ground floor and above projecting balconies, continuous round the building or supported on corbels. The flats have interior courtyards and staircases and bear a close resemblance to English versions of the 1930s. Similar examples were built in Germany and Italy though, being of three or four storeys only, were not usual in cities in the U.S.A. and Canada.

Other notable buildings of the period

ETRUSCAN

Alatri: Porta dell'Arco.
Arpino: Porta di Città.

ROMAN

Acqua Claudia, A.D. 38. One of the best examples of the aqueduct remains in the Campagna outside Rome.
Basilica Giulia, Forum Romanum, Rome, 46 B.C.
Forum of Augustus, Rome, c. 14 B.C.
Forum of Trajan, Rome, A.D. 98–112.

HERCULANEUM (Ercolano)

Houses, especially the House of the Stags.
The House of the Mosaic Atrium.
The House of Telephus.
The House of the Wooden Partition.
Baths, theatre, palaestra.

Mausoleum of Hadrian (now the Castel Sant' Angelo), Rome A.D. 135.

OSTIA

Theatre, baths, palaestra, streets and squares, especially the main street, the Decumanus Maximus, the Via della Fontana and the Piazzale delle Corporazioni, the chief square which was surrounded by offices for trade and commerce.
Apartment blocks such as the Casa di Diana and the Casa dei Dipinti.
Also individual houses and warehouses.

POMPEII

Town gates such as the Porta Ercolano and the Porta di Stabiae.
Streets like the Via dell'Abbondanza.
The main forum with its colonnade, the Temple of Jupiter, the Temple of Apollo, the Basilica and Baths.
Theatres, Odeon, amphitheatre.
Houses, especially the House of the Vettii
                    The House of Menander
                    The House of the Mysteries
                    The House of the Faun
                    The House of Pansa.
Temple of Mars Ultor, Forum of Augustus, Rome.
Temple of Minerva, Assisi, 40 B.C.
Temple of Vesta, Tivoli, 27–14 B.C.

THEATRES or AMPHITHEATRES at Capua, Fiesole and Pozzuoli.

TRIUMPHAL ARCHES AND COLUMNS

Ancona, Arch of Trajan, A.D. 113.
Benevento, Arch of Trajan, A.D. 114.
Rimini, Arch of Augustus, 27 B.C.
Rome, The Trajan Column, A.D. 114 and the Marcus Aurelius (or Antonine Column), A.D. 180.

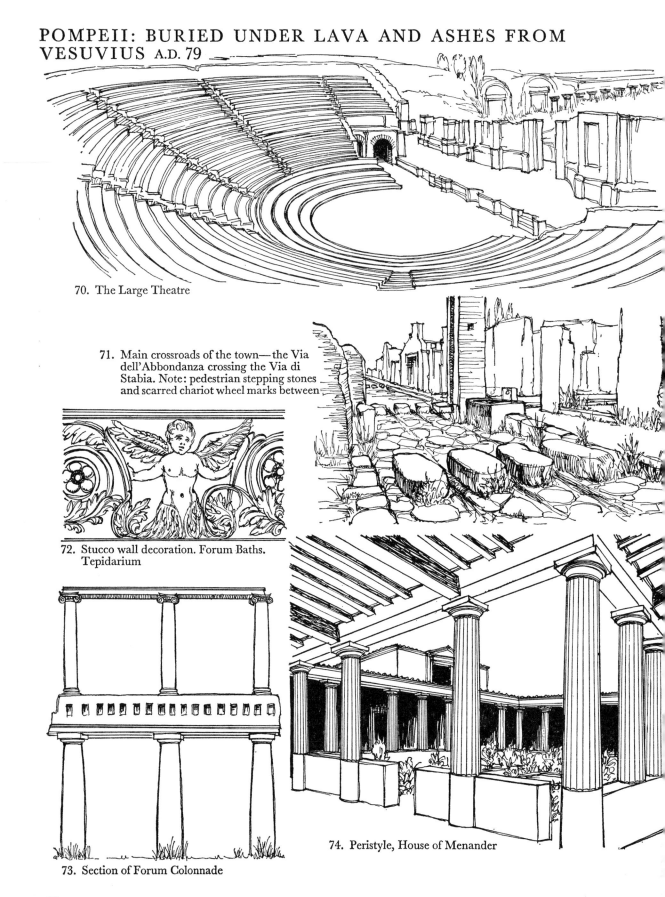

POMPEII: BURIED UNDER LAVA AND ASHES FROM VESUVIUS A.D. 79

70. The Large Theatre

71. Main crossroads of the town—the Via dell'Abbondanza crossing the Via di Stabia. Note: pedestrian stepping stones and scarred chariot wheel marks between

72. Stucco wall decoration. Forum Baths. Tepidarium

73. Section of Forum Colonnade

74. Peristyle, House of Menander

PART TWO

The Middle Ages

CHAPTER 3

Early Christian Churches
4th to 6th Century A.D.

THE Roman Emperor Constantine, by his Edict of Milan in A.D. 313, gave recognition to Christianity as the official religion of the Empire. Prior to this Christians had worshipped in secret in underground chapels and cellars. In the succeeding centuries churches were built in increasing numbers and many of the more important ones were inaugurated by Constantine himself.

Due to its simple plan, the many examples extant in Rome and other large cities and the utility of design for the Christian purpose, the basilica was accepted as a basic prototype for such churches. Later, in the eastern part of the empire, this plan gave place to the Byzantine, Greek cross variations in layout but in the west—Italy, France, England and Germany—basilicas continued to be built even till today.

The basilican form is unpretentious and practical. It is rectangular in plan and has a semicircular apse at one of the shorter sides and a narthex at the opposite one. The apse contained the altar from the beginning but this was not then necessarily orientated towards the east. The narthex usually extended along the whole width of the end of the church. It was an ante-room, colonnaded along three sides and gave on to an open court—the atrium. Some churches have lost one or both of these adjuncts but others, like *S. Paolo fuori le Mura*, still retain them (79). The church interior is divided along its length by a colonnade (with columns not piers) which creates nave and aisles. Some examples have further subdivisions giving five aisles instead of three. Earlier designs have a horizontal entablature set directly above the capitals (75, 76) while later ones, like S. Paolo, have semi-circular arches rising from the

capitals and below the entablature. There is no triforium but plain wall decorated by fresco or mosaic and, above, a row of small semi-circular headed windows. The roof was almost invariably of wood, either an open timber type (75) or a flat, panelled ceiling (76). This was painted and gilded and was most decorative; it placed little strain on the walls and necessitated no abutment. The Roman vault was almost entirely ignored in such Christian churches.

Soon developments were made. The apse to the central aisle was sometimes flanked by apses to the side aisles. Short transepts were added to some designs. The custom of building a crypt to house the remains of martyrs and saints was begun and the high altar was set above such tombs thus creating a church on two levels with the narthex end at ground level and, part-way up the church, flights of steps led downwards to the crypt and upwards to the sanctuary. *S. Lorenzo fuori le Mura* is a good example of this (75). A separate baptistery was usual at this time, a building used only for this purpose and providing for baptism by immersion. Such baptisteries were round or octagonal and were often constructed near the church in the atrium.

Early Christian churches were generally of brick, plain on the exterior but finely decorated and rich in colour within. The columns, capitals and bases were frequently taken from Roman secular buildings and one can still see where capitals do not fit their columns and vice versa. Floors were of coloured marble or mosaic, walls decorated by frescoes or mosaic pictures, roofs of painted timber and classical detail in marble. Some examples were very large and impressively decorated and most of

75. Interior. S. Lorenzo fuori le Mura, A.D. 434 and 578

76. Interior. S. Maria Maggiore, A.D. 432 remodelled 1587

1 (a). Detail. Trajan Column, Rome, A.D. 114 (*see* Page 29)

1 (b). Mosaic detail showing the Three Magi. *Temp.* Justinian. Nave arcade, S. Apollinare Nuovo, Ravenna (*see* Page 37)

2. Façade, S. Mark's Cathedral, Venice. 11th to 15th century (*see* Page 41)

these were in *Rome* itself. The greatest ones have been lost completely: *Old S. Peter's*, built A.D. 330 by Constantine, was replaced by the great basilica now standing on the same site and *S. John in Lateran* has likewise been rebuilt. Of the other two great churches, an impression can be gained of what they were like in the 5th century. *S. Maria Maggiore* has been completely altered outside but its interior, built A.D. 432–40, still retains much of the original features including the 21 bay Ionic marble colonnade with its gilded arabesque frieze. Above are Corinthian pilasters and a gold and white coffered ceiling erected in the 16th century. The floor is of white and grey marble patterned with black circles and diamonds (76). The altar is at the west end where the apse is decorated with rich gilt and coloured mosaics which cover the whole surface area and in the conch is depicted Christ and the Virgin Mary. In front is the great triumphal arch, also mosaic faced, and the Baroque baldacchino. *S. Paolo fuori le Mura*, A.D. 380 (79) (so-called as is S. Lorenzo because both great basilicas were built outside the city walls of ancient Rome) was the largest of the Roman basilicas until its destruction in 1823. It was then rebuilt exactly to the original design and today gives a clear picture of the layout and impressiveness of such churches. The vast exterior is fronted by a Corinthian colonnade and pavilions and, inside this, a very large atrium gives a magnificent view of the façade. The immense five-aisled nave is imposing with its 80 granite columns supporting the arches and cornice and, over this, is a row of circular medallions each with its painted portrait. The windows above glow because of their alabaster filling but make the interior darker than it would be with glass. The ceiling is deeply panelled, coffered and richly carved. The great triumphal arch is covered by mosaic as is also the apse. The whole interior, though doubtless closely based on the original, has,

however, none of the Early Christian or Byzantine atmosphere of the other Roman or Ravenna churches. It is vast, cold, magnificent but artificial, its detail mechanical, its mosaics pre-Raphaelite.

S. Lorenzo fuori le Mura, which was made up from the combining of two Early Christian churches, one dating from A.D. 432 and the other 578, was partly destroyed in World War II and restored in 1949. The restoration has been excellently carried out and the interior retains its Early Christian feeling with the long nave, Ionic colonnade and timber roof. The floor is at a higher level in the sanctuary where it is built over the enormous crypt beneath (75). A smaller example, but one which well retains its original character, is the church of *S. Sabina* in *Rome*, built A.D. 425, with apsidal mosaics dating from 822.

Apart from those on basilican lines a number of Early Christian churches were centrally planned and these were developed from the Roman mausoleum concept. Two particular examples exist in Rome, that of *S. Costanza*, built A.D. 320–30 on concentric double circle plan, with central dome and sloping outer roofs (77, 78), and *S. Stefano Rotondo*, built A.D. 475. The interior of S. Costanza is in good condition, with mosaics (restored) and colonnade of coupled Composite columns. The brick walls have niches, originally with mosaic covering. S. Stefano has an inner ring of Ionic columns carrying an entablature and, across the circle is a pierced dividing wall supported on two Corinthian columns. The outer walls are decorated with fresco paintings (80).

Other notable buildings of the period

CHURCHES IN ROME

S. Clemente, 4th century, rebuilt 1084.

EARLY CHRISTIAN CHURCHES IN ROME

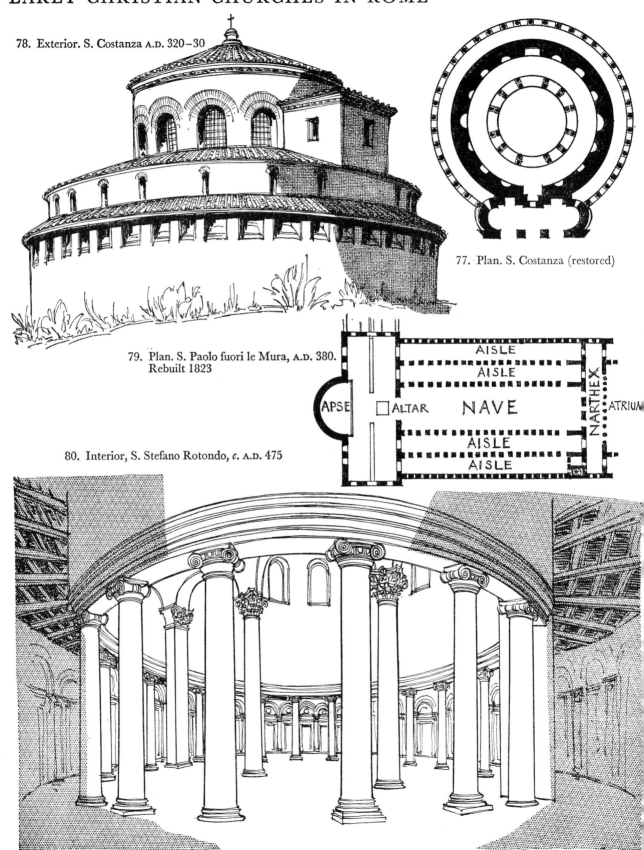

78. Exterior. S. Costanza A.D. 320–30

77. Plan. S. Costanza (restored)

79. Plan. S. Paolo fuori le Mura, A.D. 380. Rebuilt 1823

AISLE

AISLE

APSE ☐ALTAR NAVE NARTHEX ATRIUM

AISLE

AISLE

80. Interior, S. Stefano Rotondo, c. A.D. 475

CHAPTER 4

Byzantine 6th–13th Century A.D.

As early as the year A.D. 330 the Emperor Constantine transferred the Imperial seat of government to Byzantium, a small city occupying the strategic site commanding the Mediterranean and the Black Sea. He planned a new city and, when later in the century, the Roman Empire was divided into eastern and western parts, Byzantium, later Constantinople, became the capital of the eastern empire. After the collapse of the western half, Constantinople, as the remaining capital, became the centre of the empire having dominance over lands from the Euphrates to the Danube.

Byzantine architecture, though at first eclectic, being modelled on the Roman as well as designs from the east–Persia, Syria, Armenia–developed its own distinctive style which provided a basis for buildings as far apart as Russia and Italy. Remains are almost entirely of churches and monasteries and, in Italy, are restricted to two areas only: the Veneto in the north-east and Sicily in the south. The spread of Byzantine culture was greatest in its two chief periods of wealth, the first stemming from the Empire of Justinian in the 5th and 6th centuries, the second in the 11th to 13th century. Much of the work in the *Veneto* comes from the earlier period and that in *Ravenna* was initiated by Justinian himself when the city was the Italian capital of the Empire. The present *Cathedral* of *S. Mark* in *Venice*, on the other hand, dates from the second period as does also much of the *Sicilian* work. The latter is a less pure Byzantine strain, being produced under Norman control, but owing its Byzantine character to the Greek artisans from Byzantium.

Byzantine church design differed throughout the Empire but that found in Italy, not unnaturally, is strongly influenced by architectural remains from the western part of the Roman Empire and this is based upon the basilica as, for example, S. Apollinare in Classe, S. Apollinare Nuovo in Ravenna and the Cathedrals of Torcello, Grado and Aquileia. But wherever it is to be found, the Byzantine church displays certain distinct characteristics which differentiate it from Early Christian, Romanesque or Gothic buildings. The exterior is plain, almost undecorated, and very simple. It is usually of brick, ornamented with a little terracotta or marble. There is no tower (the Italian campanile is almost always of Medieval date), the atrium and narthex are often retained as is also the apsidal east end. The usual plan is cruciform, on the Greek cross pattern like S. Mark, Venice with equal length arms to the cross or with a larger western arm in a Latin cross.

The essential spirit of a Byzantine church is to be found inside. Here is mystery, semi-darkness pierced by rays of light from tiny windows and creating a shimmering effect as they fall on the mosaic surfaces which, originally, covered the whole area of the church. To give maximum effect the internal architectural forms are simplified into plain shapes providing wide, curving surfaces best suited to displaying the pictorial effect. The scenes are depicted in gold and brilliant colour over walls, vaults, domes and apses and tell the story of Christianity to an illiterate population in a similar manner to the sculptured portals of Gothic Cathedrals. The mosaic pictures are decorative adjuncts to the architectural scheme, give information in the Christian world and, by tradition, occupy specific positions in the church. For instance, the central dome simulated the vault of heaven and showed a representation of Christ Pantocrator (Ruler of All) surmounted by angels and apostles. In the drum were prophets and on the pendentives evangelists. Each part of the walls and vaults received its own quota of the Biblical story.

The Greek contribution to architectural construction had been the trabeated form, the Roman the vault and arch; the Byzantine development was the *dome*. In Byzantine churches the circular dome covers what is essentially, despite the complexity of design, a square form. The Romans had given little attention to this theme, even the Pantheon dome is supported on circular walls (81). The Byzantine architects solved the problem with the *pendentive*–the spherical triangle. Development towards this is shown below. In Fig. 81 is the circular dome set upon circular walls; in Fig. 82 an octagonal basis is provided for the circular dome by means of squinches at the four corners of the square below. A squinch is made by building a series of arches across the corners each slightly longer in diameter than the one below and projecting in front of it. Fig. 83 shows a single dome and pendentives; in such a construction the triangular spaces between the square section and the circular base of the hemisphere are built as if they are parts of a lower and larger dome so that their section is like

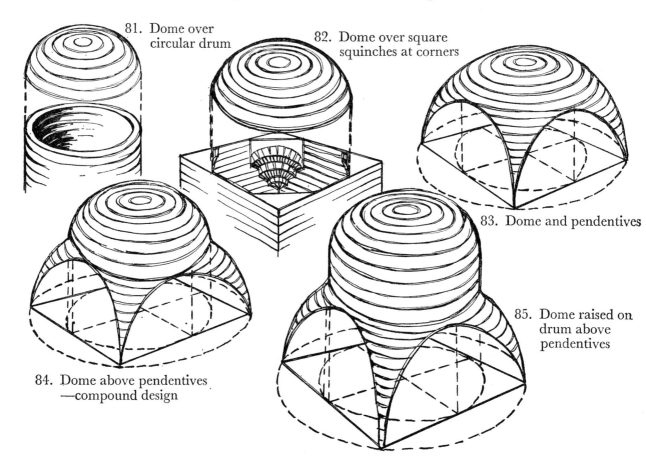

81. Dome over circular drum

82. Dome over square squinches at corners

83. Dome and pendentives

84. Dome above pendentives —compound design

85. Dome raised on drum above pendentives

DEVELOPMENT OF THE BYZANTINE DOMICAL COVERING

that of an arch carried across the diagonal of the square space to be covered. This lower dome has a horizontal section which is concentric with the plan of the intended dome. Since the lower dome is too large to fill the square space it is cut off in vertical planes formed by the four walls of the square. When the four remaining parts of the lower dome have been built high enough to give a complete circle within the walls of the square, this circle provides the base for supporting the actual dome (83). More complex constructions followed with upper domes set upon drums (84, 85). The weight of the dome is transmitted via the four pendentives to the square angles below and supported on piers from the ground.

In the north-east of Italy early churches are partly of Early Christian design and partly Byzantine. On basilican plan with a long colonnaded nave, timber roofing and prefaced by atrium and narthex, the *Cathedrals* of *Grado* and *Aquileia* are more Early Christian than Byzantine (87, 89). At Aquileia the apse is in Byzantine style and there exists an exceptional mosaic pavement dating from an earlier Roman church. *Baptisteries* like that at Grado (88) are typically octagonal outside and decorated inside with mosaic and marble facing. There are two fine examples in Ravenna. On the island of *Torcello* in the Venetian Lagoon—one of the earliest of refuges here from barbarian invaders—is the *Cathedral* and, beside it, the *Church of S. Fosca*. The latter presents a particularly Byzantine form despite later remodelling (90, 91).

In *Ravenna*, the two churches dedicated to S. Apollinare, the one in the city and that at Classe (the Roman port of Ravenna) are both basilican and were both founded under King Theodoric. *S. Apollinare Nuovo* has been greatly altered but is renowned for its magnificent mosaics covering the nave walls which show processions of Saints and scenes from the Life of Christ. *S. Apollinare* in *Classe* has retained its typical architectural form but lost much of its marble facing. Fortunately the glorious apse mosaics remain (96). *S. Vitale* is the outstanding Ravenna church. One of Justinian's own foundations, the octagonal plan contains an inner octagon (94), covered by a dome supported on squinches which are made from light-weight earthenware pots. The dome is not visible externally being covered by a timber roof (95). Inside all surfaces are faced by marble and mosaic. The portraits of Justinian, the Empress Theodora and their court retinue are world famous as are also the varied, unusual carved capitals (92, 93).

The *multi-domed Byzantine church* is less common in Italy than in the East, but Sicilian examples show plain exteriors with brightly coloured domes and have slit windows to confine the brilliant sun to shine through these at the glowing mosaics (86). A more sophisticated example is the northern Italian

86. Church of S. Giovanni degli Eremiti, Palermo, 1132

87. Grado Cathedral from the south-west.
Late 6th century. Later campanile

88. Grado Cathedral Baptistry, 6th century

89. Aquileia Cathedral. Mosaic pavement A.D. *c.* 320. Interior chiefly 9th and 11th century A.D.

90. Group comprising the Cathedral and S. Fosca at Torcello. A.D. 1008 and early 12th century

91. Narthex capital, S. Fosca, Torcello

92. Interior capital, S. Vitale, Ravenna

93. Interior of octagon, S. Vitale, Ravenna, A.D. 526–47

BYZANTINE CHURCHES IN RAVENNA

94. Ground plan. S. Vitale

95. Church of S. Vitale, 526–47 A.D.

96. Interior. S. Apollinare in Classe, A.D. 534–49

97. Basilica of S. Antonio, Padua, 1232–1307

Gothic basilica of *S. Antonio* at *Padua* which retains its seven dome plan (97). The famous *Cathedral* of *S. Mark* in *Venice* is on Greek cross plan with five domes (one over the crossing and one over each arm of the cross). This pattern is shown in the plan (99) and the view from the campanile (98). S. Mark is one of the two supreme churches of the Byzantine world. The other is S. Sophia in Istanbul, built in the earlier period, while S. Mark was begun in 1042. The third church on the site, it illustrates perfectly the amalgam of west and east which existed in Medieval Venice. Based upon the Church of the Holy Apostles in Constantinople (destroyed 1463), it appears a complicated building because its original lines have been obscured by later development. The façade, for example, in white marble and coloured mosaic is chiefly Medieval (apart from the four Greek bronze horses taken from the Hippodrome in Byzantium), but the narthex with its mosaics illustrating 1000 scenes from the Old Testament, is Byzantine. The interior, despite later alterations, is essentially Byzantine. It is richly sombre, the light from the windows of the domes playing upon the mosaics which extend continuously over all surfaces, telling the story of Old and New Testaments in hundreds of pictures.

Of the specific features in Byzantine architecture which differed from the Roman counterparts, the *capital* is the most significant. Capitals vary greatly. Classical forms were adapted, particularly Corinthian and Composite (89, 96), and here the windblown acanthus was typical. The most Byzantine form is the basket capital, decorated with plaitwork, leaves and scrolls and with deeply incised lines and drilled holes (100, 101). Many capitals were surmounted by a dosseret–a larger block placed over the capital to give a broader base to the arcade above (92, 96). Byzantine *ornament* is classical with eastern interpretation and in symbolical form.

Other notable buildings of the period

Palermo, Sicily:
  Church of S. Cataldo, 1161.
  Church of La Martorana, 1143.
Ravenna:
  The Arian Baptistery, *c.* 500.
  The Orthodox Baptistery, 449–52.
  Tomb of Galla Placidia, 5th century.
  Tomb of Theodoric, 530.

CATHEDRAL OF S. MARK, VENICE, FROM A.D. 1042

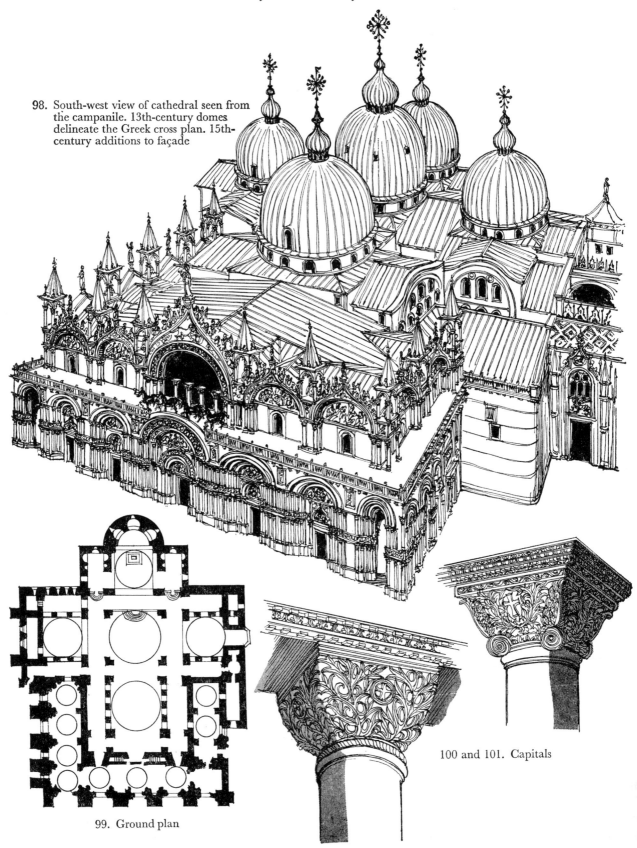

98. South-west view of cathedral seen from the campanile. 13th-century domes delineate the Greek cross plan. 15th-century additions to façade

100 and 101. Capitals

99. Ground plan

CHAPTER 5

Romanesque A.D. 1000–1250

ITALIAN architecture from these years possesses much in common with that of other countries in Europe and the work is recognisably Romanesque; nevertheless, the interpretation is markedly different from that of, for example, England, Germany or France. There are three fundamental reasons for this:

1. Climatic.
2. The unbroken influence from the Roman Empire.
3. The fact that Italy, unlike England for instance, was not one country but a number of city states, subject to differing pressures from European countries.

The hotter *climate* of Italy, with its brilliant sunshine, had a twofold effect on its architecture. Because of the warmer temperatures and the brighter sunlight, roofs were of lower pitch, not needing to throw off snow and rain to the same extent as in northern Europe and windows were smaller to exclude rather than invite the sunlight. Again, because the light was brilliant, richer colours were used on exterior decorative schemes as these reflected and were enhanced by the sunshine. Such colours were in the form of variegated marbles and glass mosaic and replaced, to a great extent, the more traditional sculptural decoration of northern Europe. The building materials in Italy, including not a great deal of stone (plentiful in England and Germany), but adequate clay for brick and a rich treasure of coloured marbles led to brick buildings with marble facings at least in the north and central areas of the peninsular.

There is no other country in Europe which was so strongly affected by the heritage left by the *Roman Empire*. In England, Germany and the Low Countries most Roman building was destroyed; in southern France considerable quantities remained but nowhere were there the immeasurable numbers of ruined and partly ruined Roman buildings that existed in Italy, even after all the barbarian invasions and depredations. Everywhere were classical columns, entablatures, sections of ornament, whole façades, vaults and pediments all giving inspiration and ideas for a new architectural form. Italian Romanesque is not Roman but the name is more accurately applied than in any other European country; it is truly of the Roman style. At the same time, the great Christian movement, vigorously asserting itself elsewhere in Europe, producing churches, cathedrals and monasteries, did this in Italy also; feudal systems arose and were established; ornament based on Christian as well as pagan beliefs can be seen side by side in one building–devils, lions, monsters–together with Corinthian and Ionic capitals, classical entablatures and deities.

The third great difference between Italian Romanesque and the English version, for example, is the *regional* one. While Italian Romanesque is different from other European styles, the architecture of the period differed even more radically from one area to another. In the north, particularly the Po valley, with Milan as its centre, was the *Lombard* Romanesque, more nearly related to German and French work on the other side of the Alps than any other Italian architecture of the time. In central Italy was the *Tuscan* or Pisan school, based closely on Ancient Rome and strongly influenced by the Papacy. In the south and in Sicily was the *Norman* Romanesque, related to our own Norman architecture, but spiced with a heady mixture of Sara-

102. Ponte Coperto (covered bridge) over River Ticino at Pavia

103. Central, wheel window. Façade. Assisi Cathedral, 12th century

104. Doorway, Pisa Baptistry, 1153–1278

105. Infidel pillar support. Façade portal. Ferrara Cathedral, *c.* 1140

106. Cathedral of SS. Mary and Donato, Murano, Apse. 1140

107. Bell tower. Abbey Church. Pomposa. 1063

cenic, Byzantine and Greek traditions. It is difficult, therefore, to study Italian Romanesque as one theme; it is better and simpler to treat it as three.

Before entering on this threefold regional description, it should be pointed out that there are a number of characteristics common to all Italian Romanesque architecture. The emphasis in Italy is generally on width and on the horizontal lines of a building rather than height. Buildings, particularly churches, are generally larger and lower than their northern European counterparts. Most ecclesiastical buildings have a separate campanile and baptistery, the church being designed as a unit in three parts. Earlier examples were built on the lines of the *Early Christian basilicas* (Chapter 3), retaining the colonnaded atrium, narthex entrance and having either no transepts or transeptal arms included within the aisle walls. After about 1100 the use of an atrium declined in importance but the traditional Italian *portico* with its columns carried on the backs of animals increased. *Arcading* was commonly used as façade or wall decoration, the east end was tri-apsidal, over the crossing was set an octagonal *cupola* and *timber roofs* were the norm rather than stone vaults. Arches were plain and generally unmoulded; classical forms of the semicircular arch prevailed.

Romanesque architecture in Italy continued later than in many European countries and was in a sense more an introduction to the Renaissance (which came much earlier here than elsewhere) than to Gothic styles.

Northern Italy: Lombard Romanesque

The name Lombard comes from the race of Langobards who were conquered by Charlemagne in the 8th century. The existing buildings of the Lombard area (chiefly the alluvial plain of the great river Po) date from a later time and are mostly of the 11th and 12th century origin. The towns along this valley flourished, however, before this time and its peoples maintained river, sea and land contacts with Spain, France and Germany, thus introducing new architectural forms to the area. The *Venetian lagoon* district on the other hand was not, in general, influenced by Lombard styles but remained under Byzantine control as exemplified by the *Cathedral of S. Mark* (Chapter 4, fig. 98). The

apses of the *Cathedral* on the Island of *Murano* (106) are a notable exception. The chief towns with Lombard Romanesque building are *Milan, Pavia, Verona*, with further important work in the district nearer the Lakes and the Alps at *Como* (the Church of S. Abbondio), *Aosta* and *Ivrea* (the cathedrals there). The chief building material of the region was brick in different shades of red, pink or brown which might be decorated and/or faced with stone or marble. Architecturally Lombard Romanesque is closer to that of northern Europe than elsewhere in Italy. Due to the region's cooler climate, roof pitches were steeper, windows larger and stone groin and rib *vaults* were used in contrast to the timber roofs of the rest of Italy. A number of these vaults, however, were built after the rest of the structure and replace wood ceilings; most examples are 12th century or later. *Arcading* was common as external wall decoration and *rose windows*, particularly on the façade, were like northern European versions, though the wheel pattern predominated. The projecting *portico* was typical, in one or more storeys with two column support to its vault under a hipped roof. The columns, as elsewhere in Italy, generally stood upon the backs of animals such as lions or bulls (109, 111, 130, 132). *Decoration* and *sculpture* in the north was less classical in inspiration than in the remainder of the peninsular and more typical of European Romanesque. However, figures, animals, devils, monsters, flora and fauna of all types were introduced, particularly in capitals (single or multi-type) (105), column decoration, bases and doorways arches and jambs. A most distinctive feature of Lombard Romanesque architecture is the tall, slender *bell-tower*, built on a square plan, unbuttressed, without sets-off and generally separated from the main body of the church. Such towers have many stages and are decorated by pilaster strips and corbel tables at each stage. The belfry openings usually increase in number of lights towards the top of the tower. A particularly fine early example is that at *Pomposa*, 1063 (107), which has nine stages.

Examples of Lombard Romanesque are illustrated on pp. 46 and 47. One of the finest of such buildings is the *Church* of *S. Ambrogio* in *Milan* which was, as it is now, the chief city of the area. A colonnaded atrium still precedes the church and there is

ROMANESQUE IN NORTHERN ITALY

108. S. Ambrogio, Milan. Atrium, c.1140

109. Lion support for column, portal, Modena Cathedral west front, 12th century

110. Baptistry, Cremona. 1167

111. South porch, Modena Cathedral. 12th century

112. Interior, S. Ambrogio, Milan, 12th century

113. Interior looking towards raised presbytery. Modena Cathedral. Begun 1099

114. Façade. S. Miniato al Monte, Florence. 1013 to 12th century

115. Column detail. Façade. Lucca Cathedral

116. Façade capital. S. Miniato

117. Façade detail, Lucca Cathedral

118. Façade capital, Lucca Cathedral

119. Façade and Campanile, Lucca Cathedral, 1196–1204

a galleried narthex. There are two towers, an older one on the south side (10th century) and a later typical example on the north (1123–8) (108). Inside, the nave is covered by domical rib vaults over its three bays and an octagonal lantern rises over the fourth. There is no clerestory and the chief illumination of the interior comes from the lantern windows. This church set the pattern for later Lombard examples; it is particularly spacious and well-proportioned (112).

Among the typical *cathedral groups* – campanile, cathedral, baptistery – in the area are those at *Cremona, Ferrara* and *Parma*. These have tall bell towers of the type described, simple galleried cathedrals and octagonal baptisteries (110). *Modena Cathedral* (111) is particularly fine, with a beautiful bell-tower, the *Torre Ghirlandina* 300 feet high, a sculptured, gabled west front with rose window and portico. Inside, the original wooden roof has been vaulted later (15th century) but the typical Lombard pattern of alternate columns and composite piers comprise the nave arcade. There are wide-arched, false triforium openings with the clerestory above giving a light interior, built throughout in warm coloured brick (113). Other good examples of Lombard Romanesque include the *Cathedral* at *Piacenza*, the *Church* of *S. Zeno* at *Verona* and that of *S. Michele* at *Pavia* which has a wall-like, characteristic façade in one gable and interesting sculptured capitals and doorways (124).

Central Italy: Tuscan and Pisan Romanesque

The architecture of this area extended from northern Tuscany to Naples but its important centres were Tuscan, particularly at *Florence, Pisa* and *Lucca*. It is an area of great mineral wealth, in stone, coloured marbles, brick and volcanic materials. The climate is warm and sunny and Tuscan architecture is famous for its brilliance of coloured marble facings in intricate patterns. The Papal influence in the region was strong and the basilican plan to churches was adhered to almost everywhere. Stone vaults were rare; decorated, coloured timber roofs were built in nearly all churches. The chief exterior decoration to buildings was in the form of arcading which extended to façades, or all round the building and included bell-towers also.

The most outstanding example of Tuscan Romanesque is the unique *cathedral group* at *Pisa*; indeed, this is the greatest Romanesque group in Italy. In characteristic plan (shown in the aerial view on page 49) are the four buildings situated in the *Piazza dei Miracoli*; the *baptistery* at the west side, the *cathedral*, the famous leaning *bell-tower* at the south-east corner and the *cemetery* on the north. The building of this group continued for a long time from the foundation of the cathedral in 1063 to the completion of the bell-tower in 1350, but the architectural style is of one inspiration and form. All the buildings are faced with marble panelling and decorated with arcading; they have weathered well and the buildings glisten in the sunshine. The *cathedral*, on basilican plan, has a double-aisled nave, transepts and apsidal east end. An oval dome is set over the crossing supported on squinches and shallow pendentives. Most of the arches are round except the triumphal arch inside which is pointed. The apse has a Byzantine richness to its mosaic decoration. The cathedral's west front (120) is magnificent, arcaded in typical Tuscan manner and the lower part is of striped and inlaid marble decoration. There is a strong classical flavour to all the columns and capitals. The west doors are early 17th century replacements to the original *Bonanno* bronze doors of 1180 but those of the *Portal of S. Ranieri* (transept) are still of this early date.

The *baptistery* is circular – 114 feet in diameter – and is covered by a later cupola. The truncated cone which extends upwards through this cupola (180 feet above ground level) is the original roof (see section in Fig. 121). The interior consists of two concentric circular forms; the outer walls in white marble, banded in grey and black and inside these an inner circle of Corinthian columns and piers. The classical influence in capitals, columns and decoration is even more marked here as can be seen in the drawing shown in Fig. 104. The pulpit by *Nicola Pisano* (1260) is magnificent. It is hexagonal and stands on seven columns, the central one of which has a base of human figures and animals, while the side columns are raised on the backs of lions. The panels depict biblical scenes.

The famous *leaning tower*, the *Torre Pendente*, is cylindrical, 52 feet in diameter, and, like the cathedral, is marble faced and arcaded, rising to six storeys. Due to insufficient foundations and uneven

3. Monreale Cathedral, Sicily (*see* Page 53)

View from the north looking inland over the mountains, showing the abbey church, begun 1174

4 (b). Façade, Orvieto Cathedral. 14th century to *c*. 1600 (*see* Page 57)

4 (a). Doorway capital detail. Façade, Pisa Cathedral, Tuscany, *c*. 1270 (*see* Page 48)

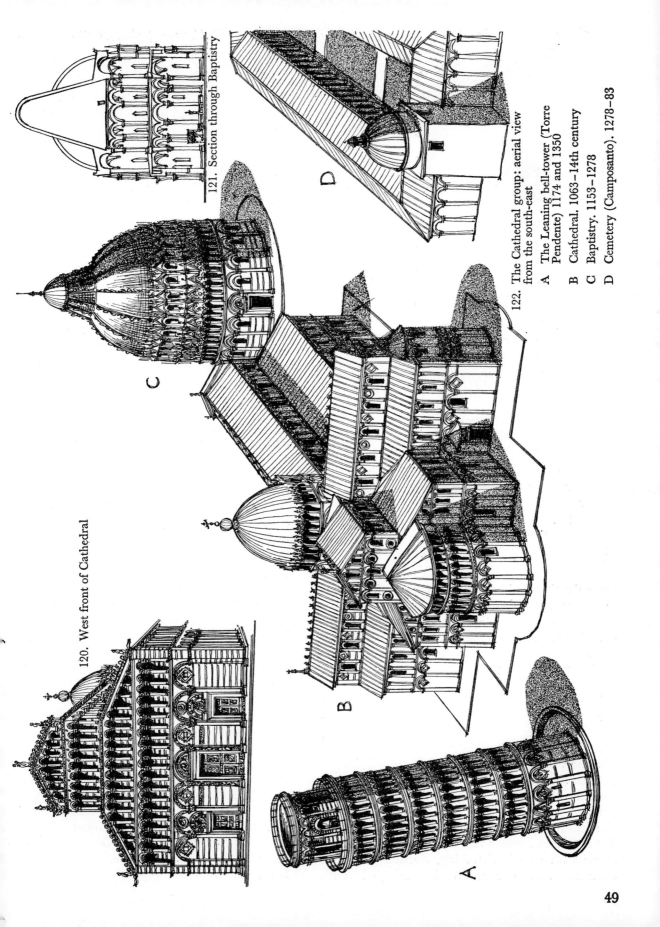

121. Section through Baptistry

120. West front of Cathedral

122. The Cathedral group: aerial view from the south-east

A The Leaning bell-tower (Torre Pendente) 1174 and 1350
B Cathedral. 1063–14th century
C Baptistry. 1153–1278
D Cemetery (Camposanto). 1278–83

49

123. Campanile, Church of S. Maria in Cosmedin, Rome, 12th century

124. Façade capitals, Church of S. Michele Pavia, 1188

ground resistance it settled even while building was in progress. It is nearly 180 feet high and over 13 feet from the perpendicular at the top. The bell-chamber was added in the 14th century. The *Campo Santo* has now been restored after the damage done during the last war but the famous frescoes are, unfortunately, almost beyond repair (122).

The magnificence of the Pisa group is such that the other beautiful examples of Tuscan Romanesque are overshadowed. There are, however, exceptionally fine buildings in Florence which, like the work in Pisa, show a Byzantine influence in their arcuation, exterior mosaics, rich colouring and marble veneers. The work in Lucca, though perhaps more vigorous and colourful is less classical in conception. The *Cathedral of S. Martino* has a Gothic interior but the exterior is Romanesque with marble sheathing, classical forms on columns and decoration intermingled with

Romanesque ones, an arcaded façade, with na thex below, and a tall, typical bell-tower (11 117, 118, 119). The *churches* of *S. Michele* and *Frediano* are only slightly less impressive; both a Romanesque and have arcaded façades ar elegant bell-towers. S. Michele shows eastern ii fluence in its decoration while S. Frediano possess a brilliantly coloured mosaic on the façade gable

In *Florence* the *Church* of *S. Miniato al Mom* perched on a hill on the edge of the town, presen a remarkably early example of mature Romanesqu style which, at the same time, is closely integrate with the traditional Ancient Roman work of tl region also the Tuscan craftsmanship in the art coloured marble veneer. The façade (114) is white marble with black and coloured banding ar patterns, mosaic decoration in the gable and Con posite columns along the lower storey (117). Insid it is designed on basilican plan in classical form ar is sheathed in marble and mosaic throughout. Tl semi-dome of the apse has a beautiful mosaic ai there is a finely designed Romanesque pulpit.

Further south the architecture is more traditio ally Romanesque and in brick and/or stone. Tl *Cathedral* at *Assisi* and that at *Spoleto* are typica each has a bell-tower at the side, a single-gable façade with one or more rose windows and roun arched doorways below (103). Spoleto has a lat narthex in front. In *Rome* is a particularly interestii church, that of *S. Maria in Cosmedin* which is very o and was developed from an ancient Roman buil ing. It has now been restored but the exteri especially retains its original characteristics. It is brick, as was normal in Rome, and has a beautif bell-tower of seven storeys, with the usual openin which have marble shafts (123). Further south still, *Amalfi* and *Salerno Cathedrals* are of interest. Amalfi has been partly rebuilt but retains a magnificent campanile and its original 11th century bronze doors to the façade. At Salerno the rectangular atrium in front of the cathedral remains with its 11th century entrance (*Porta dei Leoni*) called after the lion supports. Some of the arches are stilted showing Saracen influence from the south.

Southern Italy and Sicily

The Romanesque architecture of this region, particularly *Apulia* and *Sicily*, is unique. It displays an exciting blend of different cultures and illustrates the turbulent history of this desirable area of the Mediterranean. The cultures represented in this period of architecture are Byzantine, Greek, Saracenic and Norman. The Greeks had colonised the area (see Chapter 1); it was later absorbed into the Byzantine Empire centred in Istanbul whose best craftsmen were Greek. It was then held under Mohammedan domination and finally taken over by the Normans in the 11th century. These Normans (a different branch of the same Normans who conquered England in 1066) built the magnificent cathedrals of Apulia and Sicily in the 11th and 12th centuries but used local craftsmen who decorated them with mosaics of Byzantine style and fine sculpture by Greek carvers and constructed Saracenic arches and vaults. The Normans were a remarkable race, originating from Scandinavia (Norsemen). They settled in Northern France adapting the name to Normandy and from thence took over England, much of France and Southern Italy (including Sicily). It is interesting to compare the *cathedrals* of *Apulia*, in particular, with those in *England*. They have much in common. A study of *Durham Cathedral*, for instance, and that at *Trani* (125, 126, 128, 129) shows the same type of massive stonework, brick walls, little or no abutment, solid square towers and round-headed doorways and windows. The buildings are simple in line, large in scale, decorated by the same type of ornament. The differences are mainly for reasons of climate. In Durham, steeply pitched roofs are needed to throw off rain and snow and windows have to be large to let in adequate light. In Trani, flattish roofs are common and windows are small to exclude the

brilliant sunlight and to keep the interior cool. *Apulia*, in the 11th and 12th centuries, was still a rich land, not poor as it is today. It produced grain and wool and had magnificent ports along the Adriatic coast. The chain of cathedrals and churches built by the Normans here at *Bari, Bitonto, Troia, Trani, Molfetta, Canosa*, etc., testify to this. They are all large, solid, built of stone and marble, finely proportioned and have similar architectural characteristics: a tri-apsidal east end, rose or wheel windows in the façade, a side campanile and an impressive portal with columns supported on the backs of animals. The doors are of solid bronze, cast in Ancient Roman fashion not formed with plates attached to wood doors as in the north. The sculpture is of high quality, superior to anywhere in Italy at this time, and represents animal and plant forms, human figures being proscribed by the Moslem religion. Inside are rich mosaics and varied arch forms including stilted and Saracenic. Stone was available in quantity and fine craftsmen were there to work it and decorate it (127, 130, 131, 132).

125. West Portal, Trani Cathedral. *c.* 1180.
Original bronze doors

51

126. Trani Cathedral from the south-east. Begun 1094. Campanile restored

127. Troia Cathedral façade. Begun 1093

128. Apse window, Trani Cathedral (see A in Fig. 126)

129. South transept window, Trani Cathedral (see B in Fig. 126)

130. Column support to portal, Church of S. Nicola, Bari. 11th century

131. Bitonto Cathedral from the southwest. 1175–1200

In *Sicily*, on the north coast, are to be found the richest of these Norman foundations, at *Cefalù*, *Palermo* and *Monreale*. Here, these truly impressive cathedrals still present the brilliance of this epoch, the quality of its exceptional craftsmanship and mixed ancestry. The *Cathedral* at *Palermo* is also interesting and a very fine building but has been altered in different periods so is less typical of Romanesque than the other examples. The *Cathedral* at *Cefalù* has an impressive site almost on the sea with hills rising behind it. The exterior is, like the Apulian examples, massive, of stone, uncompromising, with tiny windows, apsidal east end and twin western towers (136). Inside are the most beautiful mosaics and a cloister displaying richly carved capitals and columns, all different and original (135). The best mosaic work is in the presbytery which displays Byzantine mosaic of high quality in traditional design and colour. All the wall and ceiling surfaces are so covered and scintillate in the restrained light from the tiny windows.

At *Monreale* is the most fabulous of these Norman monuments in the *cathedral* set in the hills above Palermo. The cloisters of the monastery church are enclosed on all four sides by coupled columns of stone and marble inlaid with brilliantly coloured glass mosaic in different patterns in the shafts and with richly varied carved capitals (133, 134 and 138). The cathedral itself possesses beautiful bronze doors, dated 1186, by *Bonanno of Pisa*, and, inside, rich mosaics on apse, walls, capitals and columns. These, like the doors, depict biblical teaching and, though not of as high standard of work as those at Cefalù and the Palermo *Cappella Palatina*, cover a vast area—some 7500 square yards. The remaining surfaces, like the lower walls and pavement, are marble faced.

The *Cappella Palatina* in *Palermo* is much smaller, being the palace chapel, not a cathedral, but it makes up for this in its quality. Here is the true blending of all the Sicilian Romanesque cultures. The ceiling is of Saracenic origin in a stalactite pattern as are also the stilted and horseshoe arches, while the decoration is in Byzantine mosaic and carved by Greek sculptors; the building itself is vigorous, solid and Norman. The interior appears at first dark after entry from the brilliant sunshine outside but, as the eyes become accustomed to this light, the rich glow of colour decoration and form asserts itself. It is a unique interior, vividly patterned on all surfaces and glowing with warmth and colour. No photograph or drawing, even in colour, can do it justice. It must be seen to be fully experienced (137).

Other notable buildings of the period

Palazzo Farsetti, Venice, 12th century.
Palazzo Loredan, Venice, 12th century.
Town of San Gimignano (near Siena): chief remaining example of a Medieval towered town, 13th and 14th century. Also, at Bologna, the Torre Asinelli, 1109 and the Torre Garisenda, 1110.

132. West porch, Bitonto Cathedral, *c.* 1200

ROMANESQUE IN SICILY

133 and 134. Capital and cloister detail, Monreale

135. Cloister capital, Cefalù

136. Cefalù Cathedral from the east, c. 1131

137. Interior, Palatine Chapel (Cappella Palatina), Palermo, 1132–40

138. Cloisters, Monreale Abbey Church from 1174

CHAPTER 6

Gothic 1250–1450

IT is sometimes said that there is no Gothic architecture in Italy, or that the Italians never understood the fundamentals of the style. Both statements are untrue and exaggerate the reality, though a study of the existing monuments illuminates the differences of concept between Gothic architecture south and north of the Alps. Partly the divergence is due to climate and, more so, to the Roman history of the Italian Peninsula. In northern Europe, France was the leading exponent, beginning in the 12th century and continuing until the Renaissance percolated there in the 16th century. England experienced a longer and fuller tradition which lasted till Tudor times. It helps to understand the fundamental differences between English and Italian work to envisage typical English examples. The purer ones are ecclesiastical: for instance, Salisbury Cathedral, typical Early English, with its simple lancet windows, soaring tower and spire and Purbeck marble shafting; Exeter Cathedral, the essence of Decorated Gothic design with geometrical tracery and complex ribbed vaults; York Minster or Henry VII's Chapel at Westminster Abbey illustrate the Perpendicular style of pinnacled buttresses, slender, panelled towers and lierne or fan vault; finally, the Tudor brickwork end product at Hampton Court Palace and the quadrangles of Oxford colleges.

Italian Gothic shows little of these features and, in this sense, it is true to say, there is no Gothic. The style, as developed north of the Alps, is rarely to be seen. The chief exception is *Milan Cathedral*, sheathed in white marble, pinnacled and sculptured all over and with some of the finest stained glass extant in its eastern windows. But Milan, started in 1385, completed in the 19th century, is

very much a German product since so many of its artists came from the other side of the Alpine ranges. Despite this, the vast cathedral (second in size only to Seville as a Medieval building) still retains Italian characteristics. These can be seen in the insistence on a geometrically based design, the emphasis on horizontal rather than vertical elements (compare this façade with York or Canterbury) and the brick construction with marble facing (139, 141). Other, fairly traditional, Gothic buildings in Italy include Abbey Churches built by the monastic orders with a basically French influence, such as the Cistercian *Abbey of Fossanova* in 13th century Burgundian style (146, 153) and the early Franciscan church of *S. Francesco* at *Assisi*. Like Fossanova, this has a plain exterior but is unusual in that it is two churches, one above the other and the interior is more richly decorated in mosaic and fresco (144, 145).

More typically Italian are buildings based on Roman and Romanesque designs, both existing in numbers all over the country. Interpretations varied from region to region according to climate and material but nowhere were dominant the vertical line, the soaring buttress and spire, the complicated stone vault. The Italians preferred to retain their timber roof where possible or a square compartment to vault the nave; they built basilican churches with a tall nave arcade, clerestory above but no triforium. They used brick, faced with marble also vivid colouring in mosaic and fresco both inside and out. Sculpture was more often in relief than in the round. The rich, ornate western screen wall was indeed only a façade; behind its great gable, which masked the aisle roofs, was a church whose construction and interior bore little

GOTHIC CATHEDRALS

139. Milan Cathedral from the north-west. Begun 1385. Façade 1616–1813

140. Plan. Florence Cathedral

141. Plan. Milan Cathedral

142. Siena Cathedral from the south-west, 1245–1380

relationship to it. The west wheel window was the chief connecting link between exterior and interior.

Most extant Medieval work is north of Rome. The eternal city lay neglected, its Popes in exile in France, while, in the south, the long Sicilo-Norman rule and culture gave way in the 13th century to Angevin, centred on Naples not Palermo; Lombard work was still very Romanesque, strongly influenced by its powerful, long tradition. The best Medieval architecture is to be found in Tuscany, south towards Rome and, of completely different derivation in the expanding empire of Venice. Characteristic were the pointed arch, vivid colour decoration in marble, mosaic and paint, carved white marble tracery and sculpture. Ornament and detail were primarily classical, even capitals were more Corinthian than Gothic while incorporating the Medieval figures and animals. Windows never reached the vast size of northern European ones (the latter would have been unsuitable for hot sunshine) (143). The deeply recessed, sculptured portals of France had no counterpart in Italy. Here, the portals were shallower and decoration was more by mosaic tympanum, relief bronze door panels and marble sculpture at the sides, as at Orvieto or Siena (142). The timber nave roofs and lower side aisle vaults required less abutment and consequently fewer pinnacles. Towers were not common and then often separate. The cupola still covered the crossing.

The finest *cathedrals* are those of *Florence, Siena* and *Orvieto*, all typifying the Tuscan approach. At *Florence* the original pattern has been altered by later work: the famous Renaissance dome and the 19th century façade. Much of the east end, the plan and parts of the interior are Medieval and work was begun by *Arnolfo di Cambio* in 1296. On the exterior the marble inlay and veneer creates an essentially classical feeling imposed on Gothic apsidal form while the Campanile, designed 1334–87 by *Giotto*, is a unique composition, but in marbled harmony with the group (140). *Siena* is the most outstanding, clad all over, exterior and interior, in black and white stripes of marble, carved richly in white marble sculpture and further ornamented with coloured mosaic and marble veneer on floor and ceiling; it is a glowing, gleaming masterpiece. The building displays a tremendous sense of space and light especially inside. Amongst so much beautiful workmanship there should specially be noted the sculptured pulpit, work of father and son, *Nicola* and *Giovanni Pisano*, who were also responsible for much of the façade (142). The hill city of *Orvieto* rises out of a flat plain and its cathedral is sited on top of the eminence, a colourful, glorious building, reminding the visitor of the days of the city's greatness. The three-gabled façade dominates the piazza in a riot of colour, gilt, bronze sculpture and white marble. It is two dimensional, constructionally and decoratively. The rest of the exterior is in plain black and white striped marble. Inside, the cathedral is simple, spacious and impressive; it is more cohesive than Siena. The magnificent west rose window is dominant (143) and sheds a golden glow to the whole interior in the evening light. Begun in 1290, the cathedral was completed in 1600.

Italian Gothic churches are less interesting and many of them have been altered later. Very much in the Tuscan Cathedral tradition, though, is the richly marbled *S. Maria della Spina* at *Pisa* (1230–1323). In different vein are two churches in *Venice: S.S. Giovanni and Paolo* and *S. Maria Gloriosa dei Frari*; both 13th century, both monastic foundations and both built in brick with only marble facings and decoration. They are typical in plan, exterior and construction (148). In *Florence* are also two examples; *S. Maria Novella* and *S. Croce*, also both of the 13th century. The former was given a new façade by Alberti in 1460. Of interest too are the *hall churches* of *Perugia* and *Todi, S. Petronio* at *Bologna* and the *Certosa* (Carthusian monastery) of *Pavia*, which is Medieval apart from its Renaissance façade.

Italy has many Medieval palaces, civic buildings, castles and bridges. The finest *palaces* are in *Venice*, mainly fronting the Grand Canal, of which the *Ca' d'Oro* (1421–36) is of the classic pattern, shown by its white marble ogee arches, its tracery, elegant balconies, arcading and roofline. World famous is

GOTHIC CHURCHES AND DETAIL

143. Façade window. Orvieto Cathedral, 1310–1600

144. Church of S. Francesco, Assisi, 1228–53

145. S. Francesco, Assisi. South porch capitals

146. Façade doorway. Abbey Church of Fossanova, 13th century

147. Doorway detail. Palazzo dei Priori. Perugia, 1284

148. SS. Giovanni and Paolo, Venice, 1234–1390 (later dome)

the *Doge's Palace*, begun in the 9th century; the present façades to S. Mark's Square and along the waterfront of the Grand Canal date from 1309–1424. In pinkly glowing, patterned brickwork and brilliant white marble carving and arcading, these elevations are the essence of Venetian Gothic architecture at its best. Stylistically they represent a fusion of Byzantium, the Orient, classical Rome and Medieval Gothic, resulting in a unique harmony (150, 152).

Medieval Italy produced a wealth of *town halls*, originally the seats of government for the city states of the peninsula. The pattern is similar though the scale varies according to importance. That at *Siena* (154), with its slender, lofty tower, castellated roof-line and Gothic fenestration is typical. Others include the *Palazzo Vecchio, Florence* (1298–1344), the *Palazzo dei Priori* (also known as the *Palazzo del Municipio*), *Perugia* (1281) (147), the *Palazzo dei Priori, Volterra* (13th century), the *Palazzo Pubblico, Montepulciano* (155) and the *Palazzo dei Consoli at Gubbio* (1332).

Castles reflect the general European trend of the 13th and 14th centuries towards concentric, symmetrical design. Two early ones belonged to the Emperor Frederick II who incorporated Roman military symmetry into the Medieval concentric defence system. This is particularly apparent at *Castel del Monte* in Basilicata; an octagon surrounding an octagonal court with eight towers on completely symmetrical plan (151). His castle at *Prato*, also a 13th century design, is larger and more rectangular. Later castles include the *Castello Nuovo* at *Naples* (1279–83), with round towers and curtain walls, the hill sited castle at *Volterra*–a massive 14th century stronghold–and the *Castello degli Estense* at *Ferrara* (149). These are all castellated, machico-lated and have or had moats surrounding the exterior walls. In Apulia, at *Lucera*, a whole hill town was enclosed in brick walls with towers which have stone quoins and window openings.

149. Castello degli Estense (Este), Ferrara, 14th century

Other notable buildings of the period

Cathedral of Palermo, Sicily, 1170–85, porch *c.* 1480. 18th century additions and alterations.

Church of S. Francesco, Assisi, 1228–53.

Houses at Viterbo, Medieval.

Loggia dei Lanzi, Florence, 1396 (now often called Loggia della Signoria).

Palazzo Contarini-Fasan, Palazzo Foscari, Palazzo Franchetti and Palazzo Pisani, all in Venice, 15th century.

Palazzo Stefano, Taormina, Sicily.

Ponte del Castello Vecchio, Verona, 1335.

Ponte Vecchio, Florence, 1345.

The Torrazzo, Cremona. The highest tower in Italy *c.* 400 feet.

150. The Doge's Palace, Venice. Grand Canal façade, 1309–1424

151. Castel del Monte, 1233–50

152. Capital, Doge's Palace

153. Nave capital, Fossanova Abbey

154. Palazzo Pubblico. Siena, 1289

155. Palazzo Pubblico, Montepulciano

PART THREE

Renaissance and Baroque

CHAPTER 7

Renaissance and Mannerism
*c.*1420–*c.*1590

THE word 'Renaissance', used by many countries of Western Europe, including ourselves, to describe the emergence of the modern world from that of the Medieval, translates, literally–as does the Italian 'Rinascimento'–into 're-birth'. This is a literal description also of the phenomenon though it only encompasses part of what happened. It is common knowledge that the Renaissance was a movement towards Humanism from pure Christianity, towards the classical forms of art and literature from the Medieval, that it began in Italy in the 14th century and spread slowly westwards. Why did it begin in the 14th century? Why did it emerge first in Italy? Most important of all, why did it occur at all?

In the story of Italian architecture, the Renaissance is the most vital of all movements and the work of this time is incomparably the greatest in the world. So thought must be given to these questions in order to comprehend this revolutionary epoch. Firstly the Renaissance began in the 14th century because it was not until that time that the climate of opinion, study and intellectual development of outstanding men was ripe for the reception and understanding of the antique world. Medieval society had largely ignored the remains–architectural, artistic and literary–of the classical civilisations. Dissatisfaction with Medieval, largely religious, answers to man's curiosity about himself, his history and his world led to rediscovery and renewed study of what had gone before the collapse of the Roman Empire. The beginnings of the new comprehension came in Italy as a natural corollary because in Italy were most of the existing remains of antique art, architecture, literature, at least, particularly the Roman part and, artistically, this

was the dominant theme of the Renaissance; appreciation of Greek work in the visual arts came much later. The third question, why did the Renaissance come at all, is more difficult to answer but it is more important to seek the reason, for here is the basis, the *raison d'être* of the movement. Since the disintegration of the ancient classical world, mankind had emerged from barbarism into Christianity. This religion in Western Europe became the foundation of all life, with intellectual thought and experience, and therefore learning, in the hands of the Church. 14th century Italy (as later in France, Germany, England) began to produce men of intellectual stature who questioned, not the importance of Christianity, but the unimportance, so far accepted, of man. In their studies of the literature of Ancient Greece and Rome they discovered a conception of man as an individual human being, important in his own right. Even though this meant conflict with the established theological ruling that man's life on earth should be subjugated to his future life after death, these scholars found themselves compelled to explore further such interesting theories. Here is the vital spark of questioning, curiosity, intellect, which divides man from the rest of the animal kingdom.

In Italy, the Renaissance began in the literary field with the studies and writings of men such as *Petrarch, Boccaccio, Dante,* all in the 14th century. Sculpture also was an early field of exploration, showing the new ideas in the work of such men as the *Pisanos,* father and son (Chapter 6, page 57). Painters followed; *Cimabue* and *Giotto,* for example. Architecture came late in the field and the first Renaissance works are by *Brunelleschi* dating from 1420. The characteristics of Early Renaissance work are totally different from Gothic and Medieval conceptions. The basis was provided by Ancient Rome but, particularly in early works, this was not a literal transcription, for buildings by Brunelleschi and *Alberti* were not fundamentally Roman. It was the next century which established under *Bramante* the pioneer Roman style. Brunelleschi was essentially a man of his own age and his work was the same but it was classical not Gothic and, almost overnight, he established a revolution from Medieval to classical. In all the arts, a fundamental difference between the Medieval work and that of the Renaissance is to be seen in the human, natural and vigorous forms. Christianity, though still a most important basis for art, was not now depicted in such a hierarchical manner nor was it the only subject. All of man's life and experience, with Christian background, became the artists' inspiration, together with nature in human, animal and landscape form.

Two vital characteristics of the Renaissance were the change of status of the artist (whether visual or literary) in the community and his versatility. The Renaissance began in Tuscany, particularly in Florence. Here, under Medici patronage, poetry, painting, sculpture and architecture flourished and the artist became one of the most important members of the community. He was in demand by all men of wealth and position to write about them, to build palaces and churches and to decorate these according to taste and means. The artist, in turn, recognised this and was sensible of his importance. Many are the documented stories of Michelangelo, for instance, turning down the commissions of an influential patron because he was not sufficiently consulted or appreciated. At the same time, artists were extremely able, versatile and cultured men, particularly the best of them. None excelled at only one art or craft. Nearly all were painters, sculptors and architects and some wrote as well or were outstanding goldsmiths, ceramic workers or tapestry designers. Thus, the first Renaissance architect of Florence Cathedral was *Giotto*, a painter and the great *Alberti* was a scholar, writer, mathematician

as well as builder of many churches. In Renaissance Italy, artists were top members of their communities and they earned that position.

Italy was pre-eminent in Europe in the arts of the Renaissance from the early 15th century beginning in Florence and moving on to Lombardy with buildings rich in marble decoration at Pavia, Milan and Bergamo, then entering the purer phase of the High Renaissance in Milan and Rome with the work of Bramante. In 16th century Venice and the surrounding area *Palladio, Sansovino* and *Sanmichele*, like *Raphael, Peruzzi, Romano* and *Michelangelo* in northern Italy and in Rome moved towards a change of interpretation and Mannerism. This word, introduced about 50 years ago, denotes the transitional work which was carried out in the later 16th century and differentiates between the High Renaissance pure classical style of Bramante and his contemporaries on the one hand and the 17th century Baroque work on the other. It is less correctly Roman than the High Renaissance, shows a restlessness of feeling and motif, a reluctance to follow too closely antique classical precepts and sometimes displays a neurotic, variable handling of movement. Mannerism shows itself in all the arts; the architectural work is discussed later in the chapter.

The similar words classical, classicism and classic are common in descriptions of architecture between 1420–1900 but they have different usages. Classical is the adjective describing designs and characteristics of the antique world of Greece and Rome. Classicism is the appropriate noun. Classic has a wider, adjectival interpretation. It is applied to designs of many different types, providing that they are based on a proven early, original style. This might be classical but could equally well be Byzantine, Romanesque or even Etruscan.

Early Renaissance: Mainly Florence

Filippo Brunelleschi (1377–1446), goldsmith and sculptor, became the first of the Renaissance architects. His work was Tuscan but, as in the antique world, his ideas were based upon a search for symmetry, proportions which were mathematically ideal in the relationship of one part or space to another. About 1425 Renaissance painters had discovered the laws of perspective. Brunelleschi developed perspective in architectural form. His first work was the *Foundling Hospital* (Ospedale degli Innocenti) begun in 1419 and the first building of

its kind in the world. His round-arched colonnade is truly Tuscan, having much in common with Tuscan Romanesque but indubitably classical in planning and detail (199, 200). His work on the *dome* of *Florence Cathedral* is well known. Here, he faced and conquered the vast problem—in 1404—of covering the 138 feet span presented by the completed drum and which was too great for available timber centering. After leaving sculpture for architecture Brunelleschi had studied mathematics and also had spent time in Rome in drawing and recording Ancient Roman buildings. His interest was aroused in creating immense vaults and domed constructions in the manner of the Roman baths. At Florence Cathedral he eventually built a dome on Gothic principles with Medieval style ribs supporting a later, light infilling. The dome is taller than a hemisphere to offset the thrust. Though, as a classicist, he would have preferred a true hemisphere, he dared not build one on the existing octagonal drum which had no exterior abutment. To retain the exterior shape and to reduce the weight there are two domes here, one exterior and one interior. The lantern, designed by Brunelleschi, was built after his death. It is large and heavy, to control the eight ribs below and forms a fitting finial to the great cathedral (156).

156. ✝ Dome and eastern apses of Florence Cathedral viewed from the top of Giotto's campanile. Dome by Brunelleschi, 1420–36, lantern, 1461

In his basilican *churches* Brunelleschi sought symmetry, a control and unity of space and achieved a great breadth and feeling of light not to be found in Medieval churches. *S. Spirito*, 1436 (161) and *S. Lorenzo*, *c.* 1420, the Medic church, are examples of this. Brunelleschii was, like so many Renaissance architects, fascinated by the concept of the centrally planned church. Used by both Greeks and Romans in temple design, this is the ultimate form in classical

157. S. Maria Novella, Florence. Façade, 1470, Alberti

158. Narthex capital. S. Maria delle Grazie, Arezzo, 1470, Benedetto da Maiano

159. Façade entablature. S. Francesco, Rimini, 1446, Alberti

160. Detail. S. Andrea

162. Detail of vault, Pazzi Chapel, Brunelleschi

163. S. Andrea, Mantua. Main doorway, 1472, Alberti

161. S. Spirito, Florence. Brunelleschi, 1436

metaphor. In the *Old Sacristy* at *S. Lorenzo* (so-called to distinguish it from Michelangelo's New Sacristy) Brunelleschi experimented with the scheme. In his unfinished *Church of S. Maria degli Angeli*, 1437, he began work on the first centrally planned Renaissance building. It has sixteen sides with eight chapels opening from an octagonal central area with domed covering. The church is still there – unfinished. His *Pazzi Chapel* (S. Croce), 1433, is more sophisticated. It contains some beautiful ceramic work by *Luca della Robbia* 1400–82) (162).

Leon Battista Alberti (1404–72), the other great 15th century architect, was born in Genoa. He was a writer with an intellectual rather than the practical approach of Brunelleschi, a great traveller and particularly interested in the mathematics and theories of classical architecture. Like Brunelleschi, he studied Ancient Roman ruins and was a sculptor. His famous books on architecture, like those of *Sebastiano Serlio*, spread Renaissance ideas and classical designs throughout Italy and beyond and had great influence on Western Europe. Alberti's *church architecture* reflects his personality. His façade to *S. Maria Novella* in *Florence*, where he solved the centuries-old problem of reconciling the differing heights of nave and aisles in façade design by the insertion of side scrolls, became the prototype for many churches. The treatment is typically Tuscan in its coloured marble veneer but correctly classical in proportion and detail (157). His *S. Francesco* (Tempio Malatestiano) at *Rimini* has another, differing, finely detailed and articulated façade (159). Probably his finest work is *S. Andrea at Mantua*, 1472 (160, 163), and certainly far ahead of its time with his handling of the crossing dome and aisleless nave. Here is a proto-Baroque method of dealing with space enclosure, not seen again until Vignola's Il Gesù (page 82). The coffered barrel vault throughout is reminiscent of Roman thermal establishments.

15th century Palaces

Italy was a country of many city states which were controlled by rich merchants and church families. These wealthy men built palaces in the city centres which still needed protective fortification and comprised living, office and warehouse accommodation. *Florentine palaces* are the prime instances and are most characteristic. The street fronts are rusticated and fortified in appearance with few, small openings on the lower floors (used for shop and warehouse quarters) while classical windows lit the living accommodation above. The strongly projecting cornice was developed. The plan is square with, inside, the open courtyard in contrast with the delicate lightness of its colonnades with arcades above. Most palaces of this time are astylar (no façade orders) but *Alberti's Palazzo Rucellai* (165), with its superimposed pilaster orders, gives a new articulation to such elevations not emulated until many years later. Famous Florentine palaces include the *Medici-Riccardi*, 1444–60, by *Michelozzo* – a prototype – the *Strozzi*, 1489, by *Benedetto da Maiano*, the *Gondi*, 1490–8, by *Giuliana da Sangallo* and the vast *Pitti Palace* (166) by, possibly Brunelleschi or Alberti, and enlarged later. This is perhaps the most typical and impressive façade of all with its vast rusticated length, a tribute to the wealth of Florentine merchants (see scale of figures, 166).

Venetian palaces of this date are not so very different from the Gothic Ca' d'Oro, though classical fenestration and detail slowly began to replace Medieval as in the *Palazzo Vendramin–Calergi* (170). One of the finest of the 15th century examples is the *Ducal Palace* at *Urbino*, set high on a hill top giving magnificent views. The courtyard, in particular, is elegantly proportioned and Florentine in execution (168).

A different type of Early Renaissance work was developed in *Lombardy* and surrounding areas. Buildings here were Renaissance more in decoration and feeling than in construction – a parallel to German and English Renaissance conceptions in

164. Palazzo Pandolfini, Raphael

165. Palazzo Rucellai, Alberti. Begun 1446

166. The Pitti Palace, begun 1458. Possibly designed by Brunelleschi or Alberti. Enlarged c. 1550

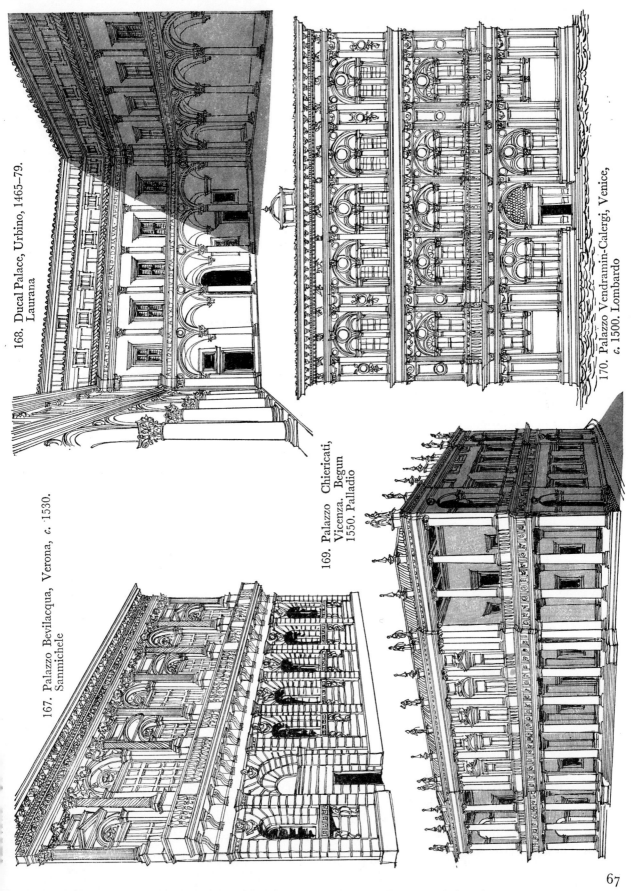

168. Ducal Palace, Urbino, 1465–79. Laurana

170. Palazzo Vendramin-Calergi, Venice, c. 1500. Lombardo

167. Palazzo Bevilacqua, Verona, c. 1530. Sanmichele

169. Palazzo Chiericati, Vicenza. Begun 1550. Palladio

67

the 16th century, though in quite different form. Typical of such north Italian work is the façade of the *Certosa di Pavia* (171, 172) and the *Colleoni Chapel* at *Bergamo* (173, 174), both by *G. A. Amadeo*. These are elaborately decorated marble buildings in rich colour and good craftsmanship. Of simpler and more genuinely Renaissance pattern are *Michelozzo's* works in *Milan*: the *Portinari Chapel*, 1462 and the *basilica* of *S. Eustorgio*. The latter has affinities with Brunelleschi's S. Lorenzo in Florence.

The High Renaissance: 16th century

This century was dominated by three men of genius so that the reputations of many other artists of ability tend to become overshadowed. These men were *Bramante, Raphael* and *Michelangelo*; none originally trained as an architect but all ended by creating buildings of great beauty and of supreme importance.

Donato d'Agnolo Lazzari, usually called *Bramante* (1444–1514), was born in Urbino and became a painter and writer of sonnets. He went to *Milan* and worked as an architect there till the city was taken by the French in 1499. In Milan, Bramante's work was mainly ecclesiastical and here he produced designs of purer Roman classical form than had hitherto been seen, such as the *cloisters* for the *Monastery of S. Ambrogio*. Of the three, the Doric Cloister (1497–8) is the most mature and illustrates Bramante's admiration for the courtyard of the Ducal Palace at Urbino, his home town.

Bramante was profoundly interested in the possibilities of centrally planned churches. He had studied Brunelleschi's schemes and was deeply influenced by Leonardo da Vinci's drawings and theories for the Greek cross centrally planned building, perfectly symmetrical and with radiating units. Bramante's first Church, *S. Maria presso S. Satiro*, is a reconstruction of a tiny 9th century building, still extant but now hemmed in by its towering modern neighbours. Inside, the coffered dome over the crossing is strongly reminiscent of Roman ones. At *S. Maria delle Grazie* (178) he added

an eastern arm to the Gothic church* whose na had been completed only 20 years before but in tot contrast to Bramante's great polygonal drum wi three subordinate apses. This was a church whi inspired many imitators from the contempora *S. Maria della Croce* at *Crema* nearby (181) to tl modern *S. Ildefonso* by *Carlo de Carli*, 1955, also Milan (285).

With the collapse of Milan, Bramante went *Rome*. It was then, at the beginning of a new centu and with his arrival that the High Renaissan really began with Rome as its centre, just Florence had been the city of Early Renaissan development. In the earlier 15th century Rome w still in decay and without real leadership. Po Sixtus IV began its restoration to fame as tl premier city of Italy. Bramante's work here con prised chiefly the *cloister* of *S. Maria della Pace*, h *Tempietto*, his commencement of the new *S. Peter* (page 75) and his *Vatican Courts*. The little templ built in the courtyard of *S. Pietro in Montorio* to ma the supposed spot of S. Peter's crucifixion, regarded, despite its small scale, as the most perfe monument to the Italian High Renaissance, en bodying in its circular form superb proportion an simplicity of undecorated architectural member It is typical of the Renaissance in its lack of concer over the combining of Christian and pagan i fluences. It commemorates a Christian event; i inspiration is the circular Roman temple. It co sists of a cylinder with peristyle and entablatu surmounted by a dome. The order is plain Tusca Doric, the proportions in such perfect harmony th it could be enlarged considerably without detr ment (177).

Bramante's lead was responsible for man centrally planned churches by other architect Apart from the one at *Crema* (181), are *S. Maria del Carceri* at *Prato* by *Giuliana da Sangallo, S. Maria Loreto, Rome* by *Antonio da Sangallo*, 1507 and, th most perfect example, the mountain church (*S. Maria della Consolazione* at *Todi* near Orvieto. Sti

* World renowned for possessing the original fresco (Leonardo's 'Last Supper'.

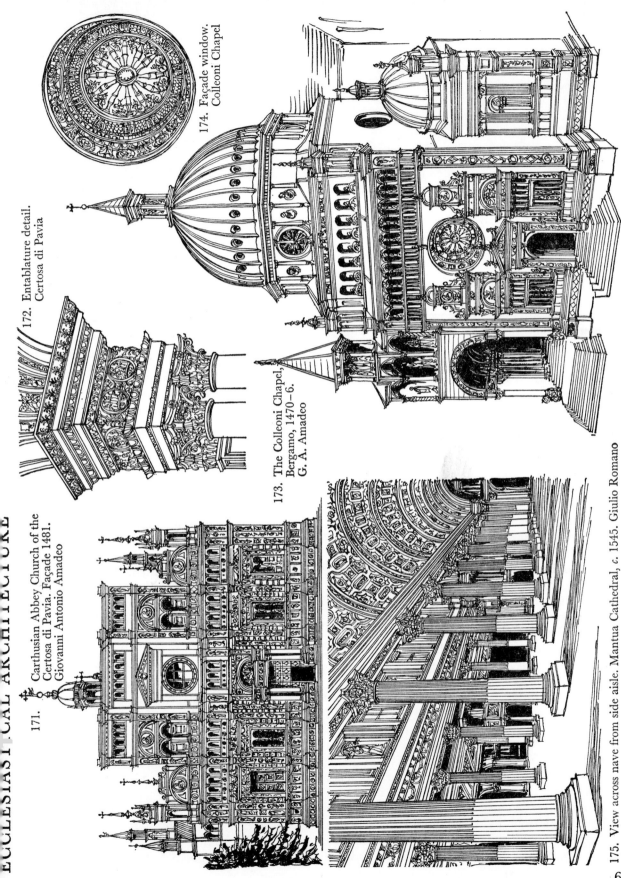

ECCLESIASTICAL ARCHITECTURE

172. Entablature detail. Certosa di Pavia

174. Façade window. Colleoni Chapel

173. The Colleoni Chapel, Bergamo, 1470–6. G. A. Amadeo

171. Carthusian Abbey Church of the Certosa di Pavia. Façade 1481. Giovanni Antonio Amadeo

175. View across nave from side aisle. Mantua Cathedral, c. 1545. Giulio Romano

in the open country, outside Todi, stands this completely symmetrical square church, an apse on all four sides and surmounted by drum and dome – the ultimate and logical result of this type of design (176, 179).

Roman Palaces and Villas 16th Century

15th century palaces in Rome had been on a different plan from those in Tuscany. Often there was no courtyard but a long, low rectangular block with interconnecting rooms. The *Palazzo Venezia* (1455) is typical. The *Palazzo della Cancelleria* (1486–96) shows Alberti's influence and marks the dawn of the High Renaissance. It has a beautiful courtyard with delicate arcades; the façades are long, low and plain with low relief pilasters (182). In the 16th century wealthy men built town houses (*palazzi*) on narrow, irregularly sited plots and, as in Ancient Rome, spacious suburban villas to relax in. The town house had a street façade and smallish interior courtyard. The villas, with room to spread, were more ambitious and on a vast scale like their Ancient Roman predecessors. Here were gardens, fountains, curved, long elevations, elegance and conditions for comfortable living. Façades of both types were frequently astylar with perhaps corner pilasters or had orders generally on the upper floors. Many famous architects designed such palaces. Styles were all classical but varied from pure High Renaissance to sophisticated Mannerist and, at the end of the century, towards academic vacuity. Outstanding architects were *Raphael, Antonio da Sangallo II, Peruzzi, Vignola* and *Romano*.

Raphael (Raffaello Sanzio 1483–1520) lived briefly but in a blaze of activity. In the last decade of his life, in Rome, his output as a painter was tremendous. In addition he was Surveyor to S. Peter's and was responsible for a number of palaces and a villa. His earlier work is in the Bramante tradition; later designs are Mannerist. Little of his architectural work exists unaltered. Among his palaces are the *Vidoni-Caffarelli*, 1515, the *Branconio dell'Aquila*, *c.* 1520 and, in *Florence*, the *Pandolfini*

(164). Most impressive was the *Villa Madama* (151? on the outskirts of Rome, built for Cardinal d Medici, later Pope Clement VII. It was neve completed but was based upon Nero's 'Golde House', with magnificent paintings and décor cor tributed by several artists.

Baldassare Peruzzi (1481–1536), like Raphae designed early in High Renaissance style and late in Mannerist form. His *Villa Farnesina* on the bank of the Tiber (1509–11) is a charming suburba example (184). It contains some magnificen frescoes by Raphael in the loggia. Peruzzi's work like Raphael's, stresses the importance of the *pian nobile*, the first floor, which was a contribution o the Italian Renaissance to domestic architectura design and was followed carefully throughou Renaissance Europe. This floor housed all th principal apartments; its ceilings were higher an its larger rooms were magnificently decorated. I contrast to the Farnesina is the *Palazzo Massimi all Colonne* (1532), an early Mannerist composition, o twin town palaces for two brothers. The façade i subtly curved and the treatment breaks most of th classical rules of proportion and handling of orders It is, however, unlike late Mannerist work successful and sophisticated.

One of the largest and most magnificent palace in Rome is the *Farnese* (begun 1514) and now th French Embassy (183). This was the work o *Antonio da Sangallo II* on true High Renaissance lines in contrast to the Massimi alle Colonne. Here is a monumental, symmetrical façade, unrusticated astylar, and with impressive fenestration. The finel articulated courtyard has three superimpose orders, Tuscan, Ionic, Corinthian, on Colosseun pattern. In mid-century, Michelangelo added th top storey with immense cornice and designed th façade entrance. This is a superb piece of work and blends, despite its more vigorous approach, witl Sangallo's palace.

In the second half of the century came the villa and palaces of *Vignola, Vasari, Ammanati* and *dell Porta*. The *Villa Giulia* (from 1550), now th Museum of Etruscan Antiquities, has a fine site in

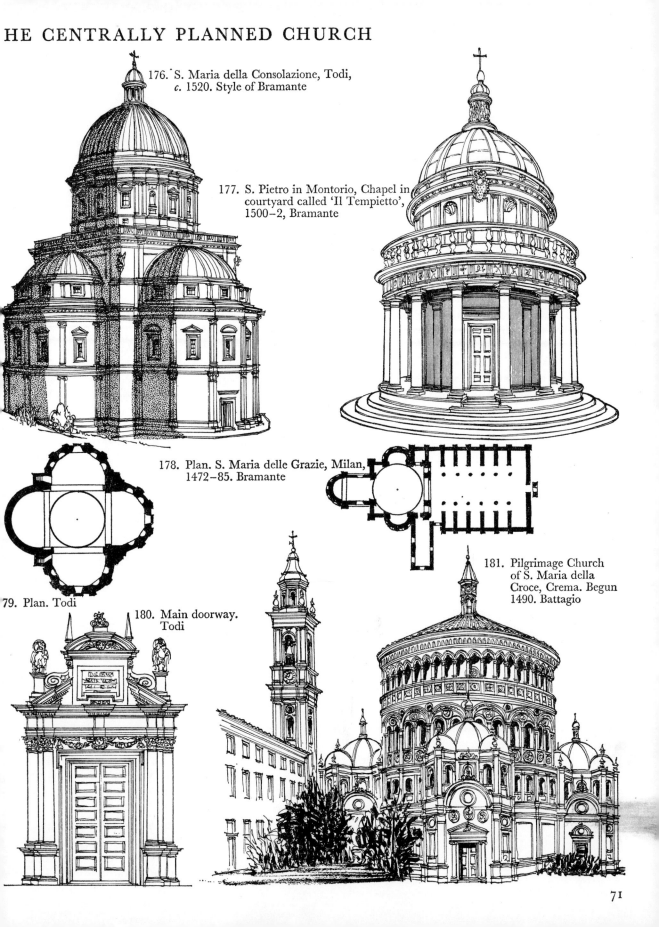

HE CENTRALLY PLANNED CHURCH

176. S. Maria della Consolazione, Todi, *c.* 1520. Style of Bramante

177. S. Pietro in Montorio, Chapel in courtyard called 'Il Tempietto', 1500–2, Bramante

178. Plan. S. Maria delle Grazie, Milan, 1472–85. Bramante

79. Plan. Todi

180. Main doorway. Todi

181. Pilgrimage Church of S. Maria della Croce, Crema. Begun 1490. Battagio

the park in Rome. A number of architects were connected on building this villa for Pope Julius, including *Vasari* and *Ammanati* but Giacomo Barocchio, generally called *da Vignola* after his birthplace (1507–73), was the prime designer. The entrance façade is austere, centred by a triumphal arch. The garden front (185, 186) is curved concavely with Ionic colonnade and has long, low wings. The garden layout and Nymphaeum (mainly by Ammanati) are in one composition with the villa and the whole presents an early instance of such a suburban scheme. Vignola's work here, at *Caprarola* on his unusual villa there, and in his first Jesuit church *Il Gesù* (page 82) all became important prototypes for others to follow. Not less strongly influential were his books, particularly those on the orders, which obtained a greater reputation than any other architectural treaties throughout the whole of Europe. One of *Giacomo della Porta's* villas (1598–1603) is in *Frascati*, near Rome, the *Villa Aldobrandini*. The architecture is simple, the sculptural decoration rich and the fountains and gardens very beautiful—a good example of his best Mannerist work.

Giulio Romano (1499–1546) was a pupil of Raphael but his work (mainly in and near Mantua) continued on the tradition of Michelangelo towards varied types of Mannerism. The *Palazzo del Te* is his masterpiece, built as a villa suburbana outside the city in 1526–31. It is an important example, its design being followed by other architects. Planned round a central courtyard the loggia and garden façades are particularly impressive with elegant decoration in stucco with panelled paintings (187). Of unusual interest are some of the painted rooms such as the windowless Room of the Giants. Romano also worked in the *Ducal Palace* in *Mantua* and the *Cathedral* (175). The latter is essentially and severely Mannerist with tunnel-like vaults and repetitive columns. A parallel in secular work is *Giorgio Vasari's* (1511–74) *Uffizi Palace* in *Florence* (1560–74).

Michelangelo Buonarroti 1475–1564

More has been written about Michelangelo tha[n] any other artist the world has ever known and ye[t] the praise showered upon him has never over[-] estimated this giant amongst Renaissance geniuse[s]. Even in his life time, and this is not usual wit[h] artists whose work was ahead of their time, h[e] commanded idolatry from his patrons, the publi[c] and his fellow artists, despite his prickly personality pride and unbending standards. He was the grea[t] force of genius leading 16th century Italian art i[n] all three forms: painting, sculpture, architectur[e]. He himself preferred to work as a sculptor bu[t] anyone who has seen his Sistine Chapel ceiling an[d] Last Judgement there cannot fail to be moved by hi[s] outstanding qualities in paint. His work as a[n] architect is less well known but of supreme import[-] ance. Much of this was carried out later in his lif[e] and though the first works in Florence might b[e] characterised as High Renaissance, the rest i[s] nearer Mannerism, even Baroque, but so personall[y] Michelangelo that it is almost impossible to classif[y] under these general labels. It is quite certain tha[t] his masterpiece, S. Peter's, laid the foundations fo[r] much of the Baroque achievements which followed

Michelangelo's architecture, like his painting always possesses a sculptural quality: never thin mean or distorted. It has power, a three-dimen[-] sional forcefulness and a combination of torture[d] movement and immemorial peace. In its rich ligh[t] and shade, its living vitality, it is the antithesi[s] of Bramante's or Alberti's academic classicism Michelangelo's architectural works in *Florence* sho[w] these qualities. The *New Sacristy* in *S. Lorenzo*, th[e] Medici Mausoleum Chapel (begun 1521), contain[s] both his sculpture and architecture. The tombs o[f] Lorenzo and Giuliano Medici with their life-siz[e] portraits above the symbolic figures of Dawn an[d] Twilight, Night and Day respectively, are the foca[l] centres of the architectural composition. The squar[e] interior is vaulted by a dome on pendentives an[d] the wall treatment is powerfully articulated i[n] High Renaissance manner though some of the rule[s]

183. Palazzo Farnese. Antonio da Sangallo, from 1514. After 1546, Michelangelo

184. Doorway. Villa Farnesina, Peruzzi, 1509–11

185. Ionic colonnade capital. Villa Giulia

182. Palazzo della Cancelleria. Interior court, 1486–96

186. Villa Giulia. Garden front. Vignola and Ammanati. Begun 1550

are bent in true Michelangelo fashion. It is a solemn, majestic, reverent interior. Also a part of the monastery of S. Lorenzo is Michelangelo's *Laurenziana Library*, begun in 1523. Here, he broke away further from the High Renaissance into Mannerist form; this is particularly notable in th· large, coupled columns in recesses, bearing no loa· and flanked by blind windows. The entrance ha͏ is tall and narrow and a feeling of power and tensio͏ is produced by the columns in their recesses. I͏

187. Loggia d'onore (atrium). Palazzo del Tè, Mantua. Architect and painter Giulio Romano, Stuccoist Primaticcio 1526–34

contrast, the library itself is long, ordered and controlled. Both parts of the scheme, entrance hall and library, complement one another in disciplined austerity.

S. Peter's Basilica, Rome 1506–1612

In 1503 Pope Julius II, newly elected, faced the problem of what to do with the nearly 1200-year-old basilica, founded originally by the Emperor Constantine, but now in a seriously dilapidated condition. Finally, with courage and determination, he decided to destroy and rebuild this Mother Church of the Roman Catholic faith and commissioned *Bramante* to design a contemporary basilica. The architect, with the Pope's approval, planned a vast, domed building on Greek cross plan, completely symmetrical, with apses on each arm of the cross: in essence, Bramante's cherished ideal, a centrally planned church (189). The Pope laid the first stone in 1506 but, at Bramante's death in 1514, little had been achieved, and the four crossing piers proved inadequate to support the vast, projected dome and had to be rebuilt by his successors.

Between 1514 and 1547 when Michelangelo took over the task, a number of architects were entrusted with the Surveyorship of S. Peter's. Not a great deal was accomplished for a variety of reasons. The architects, who all contributed something, included *Peruzzi, Giuliano da Sangallo, Raphael* and *Antonio da Sangallo.*

The last 30 years of *Michelangelo's* life were spent in Rome and he regarded S. Peter's as his most important commission, refusing any salary and working on the building till his death at the age of 89. He greatly admired Bramante's central plan and, with modifications retained it, simplifying the small compartments into fewer, larger ones, strengthening the crossing piers and making the building stable and permanent (188). As a good sculptor, he made a clay model of the building and translated this into wood. His S. Peter's is vast, but so beautifully proportioned in one part to another that, as at the Parthenon, one does not realize its size until one compares its scale to that of a human

being. Michelangelo's S. Peter's is surrounded by a giant Corinthian Order in pilaster form, each 100 feet high, surmounted by a 32 foot high attic. The whole forms a podium on which the great drum and dome rest. The drum repeats the attic pattern and the central dome is cozened by four smaller domes erected between the crossing arms. The subject of the dome of S. Peter's is a controversial one. Michelangelo designed a true, Roman, hemispherical dome like the Pantheon but, facing similar problems to Brunelleschi at Florence, he had to support this on piers making a square space not on circular walls as at the Pantheon. Constructional problems were great and the final dome is taller than a hemisphere though not so much so as at Florence. Also like Brunelleschi, he designed two shells, an inner and outer, both hemispherical. The final exterior dome is not hemispherical and thus not concentric with the inner; it is some 20 feet higher. When Michelangelo died the building was largely complete except for the eastern arm–the nave–and the dome above the drum. The dome was completed in 1587–90 by *Giacomo della Porta* (1540–1602) and *Domenico Fontana* (1543–1607) but, whether to Michelangelo's altered designs or to their own amended pattern, is a matter for conjecture. The evidence, such as it is, is contained in Michelangelo's one-fifth full size scale wooden model of the dome, made in 1561 (hemispherical exterior dome) and a taller version shown in a drawing in the Ashmolean Museum in Oxford, by Michelangelo but not verified as for S. Peter's. Basically it is perhaps an academic point. Constructionally the dome is sound; both internally and externally it is the finest dome design in the world: its span is 137 feet and its exterior cross stands 452 feet above the pavement (190).

The *interior of S. Peter's* is, apart from the eastern end of the nave, also mainly by Michelangelo. Architecturally it is simple in its coffered and panelled barrel vaults, vast crossing dome and drum supported on pendentives which in turn stand on the four great crossing piers. Transepts and west end are apsidal. Despite the lengthening of the nave

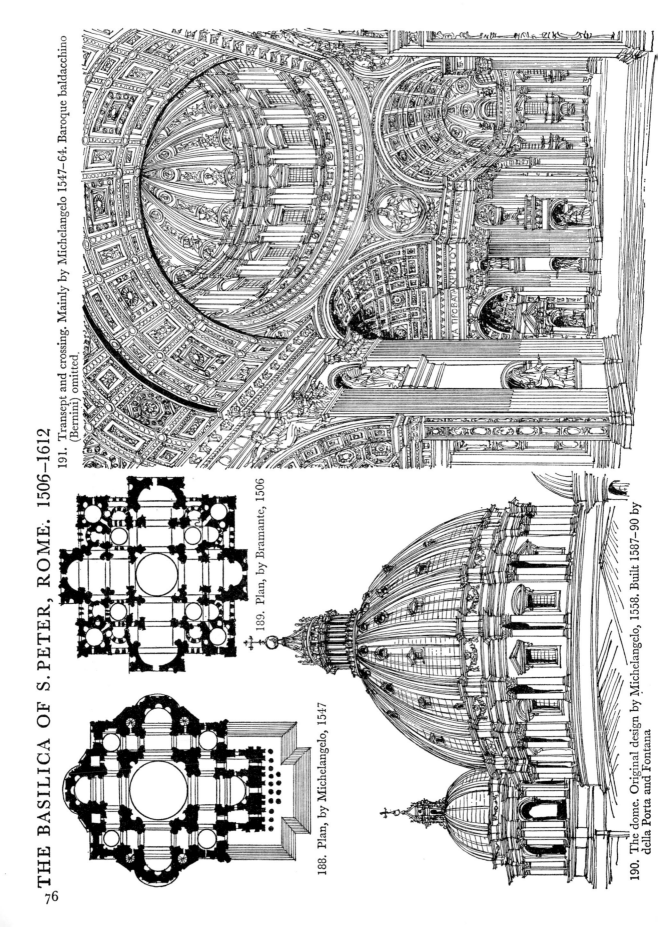

THE BASILICA OF S. PETER, ROME. 1506–1612

191. Transept and crossing. Mainly by Michelangelo 1547–64. Baroque baldacchino (Bernini) omitted.

189. Plan, by Bramante, 1506

188. Plan, by Michelangelo, 1547

190. The dome. Original design by Michelangelo, 1558. Built 1587–90 by della Porta and Fontana

76

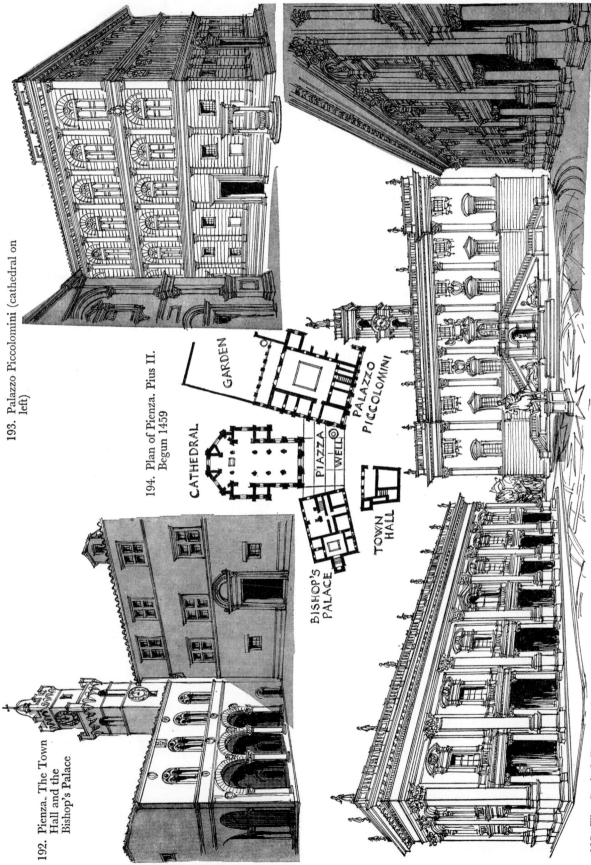

RENAISSANCE TOWN PLANNING

193. Palazzo Piccolomini (cathedral on left)

192. Pienza. The Town Hall and the Bishop's Palace

194. Plan of Pienza. Pius II. Begun 1459

GARDEN

CATHEDRAL

PIAZZA

WELL

PALAZZO PICCOLOMINI

BISHOP'S PALACE

TOWN HALL

195. The Capitol, Rome, including the Palazzo Capitolino, Palazzo del Senatore and the Palazzo dei Conservatori 1540–1644. Designed by Michelangelo

arm into a Latin cross in the early 17th century, the cathedral is still of one type of design – a remarkable achievement for a building begun in 1506 and not finished till 1612. This is in greater part due to the brilliance and industry of Michelangelo (191).

Renaissance Town Planning

Revival of interest in planning towns specifically on an architectural basis not only expediency, came with Renaissance rediscovery of Ancient Roman designs. *Alberti* was an early experimenter, using geometrical shapes in a radial pattern. Antonio Averlino, generally called *Il Filarete*, carried the idea further, producing his plan for the ideal town which he called Sforzinda after his patron family of Sforza. This was circular with 16 roads radiating from a centre and with a ring road part way. Other designers followed suit and one example actually built was that of *Palmanova* near Trieste (1590–3) by *Vincenzo Scamozzi* who here developed the Roman grid plan on a nine point scheme. New cities were rare in accomplishment but *piazze* were developed in existing towns as at *Verona* (Piazza dei Signori) and *Venice* (the two adjacent *piazze* of S. Marco). Symmetry was the key note of all of these.

Two layouts are of particular note: the new town centre of Pienza and the Capitol in Rome. *Pienza* was the creation of Pope Pius II (elected 1458) who planned a rebuilding of his own village and called it after himself. A small town, between Arezzo and Orvieto, it appears to have altered little since Pius II's day. The centre of the town is planned round a *piazza* with cathedral, town hall and palaces (194). The Town Hall is still rather Medieval in appearance though with classical detail but the Palazzo Piccolomini bears a resemblance to Alberti's Palazzo Rucellai in Florence (192, 193).

Michelangelo undertook the redesigning of the *Capitol Hill* (Piazza del Campidoglio) in *Rome* in 1540. This had been the site for the centre of government since the days of Ancient Rome and when, in 1538, the equestrian statue of Marcus Aurelius was moved there (under the impression that it was of Constantine) it was decided to make a worthy setting for this rare Roman monument. Work was begun in 1546 but completed after Michelangelo's death by *Giacomo della Porta*, largely to the original architect's plans. The layout was for three palaces, one on each side of the *piazza* with the steps, ascending the hill from the plain below on the open, narrower side opposite the central Palazzo del Senatore. Michelangelo designed an oval pavement pattern* to emphasise the slightly trapezoidal plan of his piazza. The most important architectural feature in the palace façades is the first use of the giant order spanning two storeys which was one of Michelangelo's innovations and was employed extensively in later buildings especially in Italy, France and England. The whole complex is on Mannerist lines and is one of the few layouts existing from this century which comprise the handling of several buildings rather than just one (195).

The Veneto

Sansovino, Sanmichele, Palladio, Scamozzi

This area of north-eastern Italy, living under the domination of the Venetian Republic, had always been different in its artistic interpretations of current trends, due to its close mercantile connections with Constantinople, Dalmatia and the East. 15th century palaces continued to have semi-Gothic façades (page 65) and, in Venice itself, there was no need of, or room for, arcaded courtyards – the arcades were on the canal fronts for all to see. Work nearer to Renaissance lines, though still reflecting Venice's cultural isolation, can be seen in the *Scuola di San Rocco* (1520–50), now the city hospital, and in the *Church of S. Zaccaria* (1458–1515) by *Pietro Lombardo*. After the collapse of Rome in 1527, a number of artists came north-eastwards and Venetian architecture showed more of the Renaissance revolution. Two such artists were Jacopo Tatti, called *Il Sansovino* (1486–1570) and *Michele Sanmichele* (1484–1559). *Sansovino*, a Floren-

* Not the existing pavement.

78

196. Library of S. Mark, Venice. Sansovino, 1536–53

198. Entablature and parapet, library of S. Mark, Venice

197. Porta Palio, Verona, Sanmichele, mid-16th century

199. Capital, Foundling Hospital, Florence

200. Foundling Hospital, Florence, 1419–45, Brunelleschi

tine, originally a sculptor, carried out both architectural and sculptural work in *Venice*; both show the influence of Michelangelo in their power and close relationship in one building. His greatest achievement is the *Library of S. Mark* (Biblioteca Sansoviniana). It is a rich, beautifully articulated work of the late Renaissance, fittingly sited in the Piazzetta S. Marco opposite the Doge's Palace (196, 198). Next to it, along the waterfront, is his *Zecca* (the Mint), 1537–45, while, in the Piazzetta was his *Loggia del Campanile*. A magnificent sculptural work, this had to be replaced in 1902 with the collapse of the campanile. He was responsible for a number of Venetian palaces of which the most outstanding is the *Palazzo Cornaro* (now the Prefettura, 201). This is three-storeyed and has the traditional different super-imposed orders. It set a pattern for Venetian palace design until the late 17th century.

Sanmichele was a Veronese and, after many years in Orvieto and Rome, returned to *Verona* where he was given the task of handling the city's fortification. In this connection he built a series of monumental *city gates* (197). Among his *palaces* are the *Canossa* and the *Pompei* with, best known, the *Bevilacqua* (167). In this building, like Sansovino's library, he succeeded in combining the Venetian love of decoration and rich sculpture with the solid qualities of Rome.

The most influential architect of the Veneto in the 16th century was *Andrea*

Palladio (1508–80, Andrea di Pietro della Gondoa) Palladio's work like that of Alberti and Michelangelo, profoundly affected architects of other nations in other ages as well as those of his own. A notable instance of this is the 18th century school of English architecture (Palladian) founded particularly on his principles as well as Inigo Jones' first English Renaissance works which owed much to him. All his life Palladio strove to pattern his crea

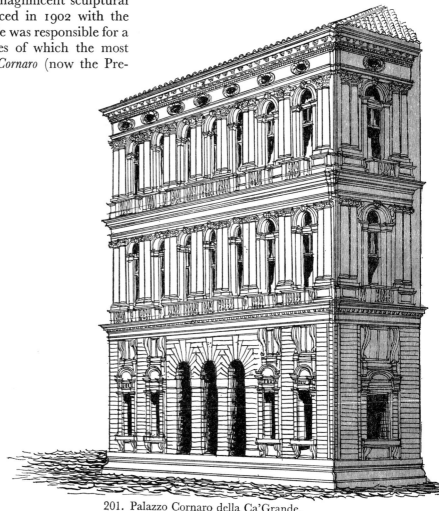

201. Palazzo Cornaro della Ca'Grande, Venice, Sansovino. Begun 1537

5. View of the south transept from the north aisle of the nave. Siena Cathedral. Predominantly black and white marble. 14th and 15th centuries (*see* Page 57)

6 (a). Detail panel from the bronze (east) doors of the Baptistery, Florence ('the Gates of Paradise'). Lorenzo Ghiberti, 1425–52

6 (b). The Medici Chapel, S. Lorenzo, Florence. Michelangelo, 1520–34. This detail shows the tomb of Giuliano de'Medici, with Giuliano in the centre and, below, the reclining symbolic figures of 'Night' and 'Day' (*see* Page 72)

202. View of the Villa Capra, nr. Vicenza. Begun 1567. Palladio

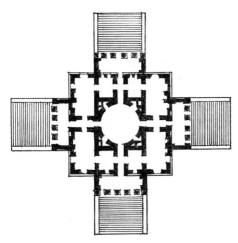

203. Plan. Villa Capra

ions on the original Roman manner. He made
hundreds of drawings of Roman monuments in
Rome and as far afield as Dalmatia and Provence,
and he closely studied Vitruvius' books on architecture. He made drawings for a number of publi-
cations but his '*I Quattro Libri dell'Architettura*' and
'*L'Antichità di Roma*' were translated into many
languages and provided the basis for Renaissance
building all over Europe.

Palladio's own architectural style was influenced
by the pure classicism of Bramante but also took a
vivid Mannerism from Michelangelo and Vignola.
He designed many buildings—civic architecture,
palaces and villas also churches—most of which are
in Vicenza and Venice. His notable civic work is the

replanning of the *Town Hall* of *Vicenza*, 1549 (the
Basilica) where he established a pattern in his
handling of the two superimposed orders, Doric
and Ionic, with entablatures broken forward over
each column, accentuating these instead of giving
the uninterrupted horizontal emphasis like
Sansovino's library. In all his numerous and varied
designs for palaces and villas Palladio based them
on what he thought the Roman pattern would have
been and was careful to create a symmetrical,
imposing and vital effect. Two examples, one in
town, one in the country, suffice to show these
characteristics. In *Vicenza*, the *Palazzo Chiericati*
(169) brings the loggia and arcade (generally
confined to palace courtyards) on to the façade.
For emphasis, he steps forward the central mass
but otherwise, the traditional Doric below Ionic
above orders are retained with unbroken entablatures. The palace is a finely balanced instance of
his art, well handled in its pattern of light and
shade, mass and detail. Other town palaces in
Vicenza include the *Thiene*, the *Valmarana* and the
Porto, all of similar date. Among his *villas*, the *Villa
Capra* (the Rotonda) is the best known and at least
two interpretations remain from Palladian England—Lord Burlington's Chiswick House and
Campbell's Mereworth Castle. The Villa Capra
(just outside Vicenza) is completely symmetrical
in plan (203) with central, domed hall and the
whole *piano nobile* raised on a square podium and
with four identical porticoes, one to each side. This

F

is the ultimate in symmetrical house design (corresponding ecclesiastically to Bramante's Tempietto or S. Maria at Todi) and, though probably not very practical domestically, is satisfying and effective (202). Other Palladian villas nearby include the *Malcontenta* and the *Godi*.

Vincenzo Scamozzi (1552–1616) was a pupil of Palladio and carried on the same tradition, completing some of Palladio's work after his death. He published his own work '*Idea dell' Architettura Universale*' in 1615 (also page 78).

Churches of the Later 16th Century

Palladio, Vignola, della Porta, Fontana

Church design evolved between 1560 and the end of the century. *Palladio's churches, in Venice*, were based, as he was convinced, on Roman temple pattern, especially the façades where he established the scheme of two or more interpenetrating orders with their entablatures and pediments. At *S. Giorgio Maggiore* there are two such units and, in this way, the age-old difficulty relating the façade design to the differing heights of aisles and nave (Gothic, page 57) (Alberti, page 65) is solved here by different orders and pediments, the nave member being higher (206). At *Il Redentore*, also in Venice, there are three such pediments and units, the third being found within the nave compartment of the temple front.

With *Vignola, della Porta* and *Fontana* came the break through which pointed the way to Baroque churches. The Mother Church for the Society of Jesus, founded in 1540, *Il Gesù*, was commissioned to be built in Rome. This great church, most influential in architectural design for several hundred years, was begun in 1568 under its architect *Giacomo da Vignola* (1507–73). His terms of reference stated that the church must be able to hold a large congregation all of whom must be able to hear the preacher*. Vignola designed a church

---

* A similar problem faced Wren in designing his 17th-century city churches to replace those lost in the Great Fire of London.

with a wide, short, barrel vaulted nave and shallow transepts to give space and good acoustics. There are no aisles or colonnades, only side chapels, thus creating spaciousness and dignity. To make up for the lack of side aisle lighting, the architect provided a large dome with fenestrated drum which flood the whole church dramatically with light and give a unity and sense of space hitherto unknown in Gothic or Renaissance churches built on the Latin cross plan (204, 205). Vignola died in 1573 when the work had reached cornice level. The façade was built by *Giacomo della Porta*, who had carried out a great deal of ecclesiastical work including completing the dome of S. Peter's, with *Domenico Fontana*. He created the façade of Il Gesù partly to Vignola's designs and used side scrolls between nave and aisle levels in Alberti's classic manner (207). The present interior of Il Gesù was altered in the 17th and 19th centuries but, despite this, it became the pattern for churches all over Europe, especially Jesuit ones and marks the crossroads between Mannerism and Baroque.

Other notable buildings of the period

Como Cathedral, late 15th century. Mixed Medieval and Renaissance elements.
Church of S. Anastasia dei Greci, Rome, della Porta late 16th century.
Church of S. Anna dei Polafrenieri, Rome, Vignola 1572.
Church of S. Maria di Carignano, Genoa, Alessi, 1552
Church of S. Maria di Loreto, Rome, da Sangallo and, later, del Duca, *c.* 1580.
Church of S. Sebastiano, Mantua, Alberti, begun 1460 but not completed.
Loggia del Capitano, Vicenza, Palladio, 1571.
Palazzo Corner-Spinelli, Venice, *c.* 1480.
Palazzo del Consiglio, Verona, 1476–93.
Palazzo Grimoni, Venice, Sanmichele, 1549.
Palazzo Pazzi-Quaratesi, Florence, *c.* 1470. Decorative sculpture by Giuliano and Benedetto da Maiano.
Ponte S. Trinità (Arno) Florence, Ammanati, 1566–1569. (Destroyed 1944 but now reconstructed.)
Villa d'Este, Tivoli, mid-16th century.
Villa Garzone, Pontecasale, Sansovino, *c.* 1540.

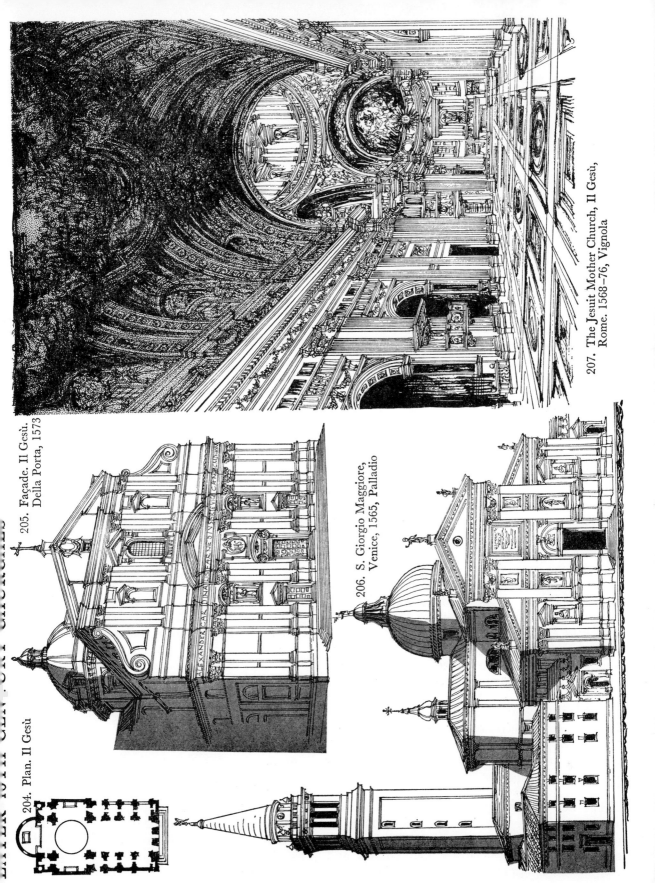

207. The Jesuit Mother Church, Il Gesù, Rome. 1568–76, Vignola

205. Façade. Il Gesù.
Della Porta, 1573

206. S. Giorgio Maggiore,
Venice, 1565, Palladio

204. Plan. Il Gesù

CHAPTER 8

Baroque *c.* 1590–*c.* 1780

Iт is less than a century since architectural historians recognised Baroque as an art form in its own right, differing from both Renaissance and Mannerism. The word used to describe it was applied, in the first instance, as a term of disapprobation to indicate criticism of what was thought to be simply a late Renaissance development characterised by exuberance decadence. It comes from the Portuguese word *barroco* (or Spanish *barrueco*) used by fishermen to denote a mis-shapen pearl. This derogatory appellation, stemming from the accentuated curves of the style, is paralleled by the similar mis-naming of 'Gothic' architecture by Vasari, indicating contemptuously his dismissal of what he and his contemporaries thought a barbarian art form.

The underlying force of the Baroque movement was, like the Renaissance, based on a new process of thinking but, whereas the Renaissance was a revival of Humanism in revolt against a too rigid Medieval Christian straitjacket the Baroque stemmed from the Counter-Reformation which was a turning away from Humanism back to the Catholic Church. It was realised that there was a deep need for a re-introduction of spiritual values and orders like the Jesuits helped to re-establish a Christian way of life more suited than the Medieval one to the modern world. The movement back to Christianity had begun in the mid-16th century; by the 17th it had become organised and its leaders appreciated that, to provide for the spiritual needs of the people it must appeal to everyone.

The new art form which developed from the Renaissance, through Mannerism, into Baroque used all media – architecture, sculpture, painting, music, literature – to make the Church real and vital to all. Baroque architecture is, like that of the Renaissance, entirely classical in concept, usin; the orders constructionally and decoratively, an all classical ornament. Its interpretation of thes is much freer with the use of curves, not only in ceiling design, but in whole walls, alternatin; sinuously from concave to convex. The whol appearance is of vitality and movement; to this i added dramatic lighting effects from only one o two sources – comparable to a Rembrandt painting The dynamic quality of Baroque is accentuated b broken pediments, entablatures and column separate and broken forward and the incorporatio of vital, naturalistic sculpture and painting in on unit with the architectural design. The favourit plan is oval, demonstrating the maximum qualit of movement and this is echoed in the ceiling abov which pulses with warmth and richness of colour a colour which appears in architecture also i different marbles and mosaics.

There is no parallel to Italian Baroque i England or northern Europe. It is suited primaril to the southern, Latin and Catholic peoples; i spread to southern Germany, Austria and Switzer land where it was dominant for a long time. As th 18th century succeeded the 17th and the Frencl influence superseded Italian Baroque, the tw forms of the English Classic Revival and the Frencl Rococo came nearer together.

Rome

Early Baroque 1590-1625

Carlo Maderna (1556–1629) was one of the firs of the Baroque architects to break away from th academic Mannerism which dominated Roma architecture in the last years of the 16th century His work was forceful and vigorous, his façade

208. Cathedral of S. Pietro, Bologna, 1605. Magenta and Ambrosini

209. Façade doorway. S. Maria della Vittoria, Rome, Soria, 1624–6

210. The New Cathedral, Brescia. Begun 1604, Lontana, Rotunda 11th century, Dome, 1825

211. S. Susanna, Rome, façade, 1593–1605, Carlo Maderna

212. Façade detail, S. Maria della Vittoria

three-dimensional and sculptural and, in this, reflected the influence of Michelangelo. In 1603 he was appointed architect to *S. Peter's* which was not only a landmark in his own career but took the completion of the great basilica a further decisive stage. Little had been accomplished, except the finishing of his dome, since Michelangelo's death and it fell to Maderna to alter his centralised plan, lengthen the nave to a Latin cross form and so obscure for ever a proper view of the dome from the piazza. Maderna was most unwilling to alter the original scheme but he was over-ruled by the Pope who wanted the extra space that the new plan would give so, as again 50 years later at S. Paul's in London, the clergy must bear the responsibility for expedience taking precedence over aesthetics. The nave was lengthened by three bays, the façade was completed and S. Peter's was consecrated in 1624. Maderna was restricted to Michelangelo's original articulation inside the new nave and it was built with the vault, pilasters and side chapels in keeping with the rest of the basilica. The façade is bold and well planned and, again, Michelangelo's giant order, articulation and attic were retained. Despite the vast piazza laid out later by Bernini so that the basilica could be viewed as it was approached from a distance, all integration between the dome and the façade has disappeared; inevitably the latter truncates the view of the former (214).

A new wave of *church* building followed the establishment of the Counter-Reformation movement. The first church to be erected according to developing needs was Vignola's II Gesù (page 83), the Mother Church of the Jesuit Order. Here, for the first time, was an open interior, uninterrupted by piers or columns, and with dramatic lighting controlled from the cupola windows. The next step forward was *S. Susanna*, to which Maderna added the façade in 1595–1603 (211). It was the first proper Baroque façade in Rome and became the pattern for many churches. The design is based on a progression of architectural members in bays and orders towards a central theme. The wall projects in three steps with wider bays towards the centre. The upper stage reflects the tower and side scrolls mark the junction. The façade has unity despite strong articulation and rich handling. The

church next door to S. Susanna, very much its twin, is *S. Maria della Vittoria* 1624–6 (208, 212), the best work by *Giovanni Soria* (1581–1651). The interior is by Maderna apart from the famous Cornaro Chapel sculpture by Bernini. Maderna also completed and enlarged *S. Andrea della Valle* in 1608 (213). This is typical of Roman Early Baroque and shows Maderna at his best. The dome is high and majestic, based on Michelangelo's at S. Peter's, though not so well lit. The cupola ceiling bears an impressive painting of the Ascension by Lanfranco. The façade was not completed till later (page 91).

High Baroque 1625–75

Gianlorenzo Bernini 1598–1680

In whatever age Bernini had lived his genius would have become apparent but his particular abilities and his personality were made to measure for the time of High Baroque in Rome. Towering far above all artists of this time he dominated his world for 50 years, creating achievement after achievement with consummate ease, concentration and energy. Only Michelangelo was ever respected and revered by his contemporaries more and Bernini was to the Baroque what Michelangelo had been to the Renaissance. The two giants had much in common: they were both strong personalities and of deep religious conviction; they both lived long lives, master of their own artistic circle to the end; they were both painters, architects and poets but regarded sculpture as the most rewarding of the arts; they were both magnificent craftsmen, perfectionists and would permit nothing to turn them away from the work in hand. In personality, though, they were opposites. Bernini was a Neapolitan with all the charm and gaiety of his race, a happy husband and father who got on well with everyone; a contrast indeed to the proud, introspective Michelangelo.

The art of the High Baroque evolved beyond the serious, more austere Early Baroque Counter-Reformation. Gaiety and pageantry were adopted by the Church to attract and keep their flock faithful and Bernini was just the man to appeal to these characteristics in the Latin peoples. The drama and vividness of all his work made a tremendous impact; it could not be ignored. His sculpture, in particular, portrayed an expression or a movement of the instant, captured and held it, vital as a snapshot. He became the centre of a school of artists, architects, painters, sculptors and Rome the centre of Europe, cradle of the Baroque and the inspiration of the Catholic faith.

Bernini's architecture was, like Michelangelo's,

213. S. Andrea della Valle, Rome, 1591–1623. Giacomo della Porta and Carlo Maderna

214. The façade (facing east) by Carlo Maderna, 1607–12. Dome by Michelangelo built 1585–9. Piazza Colonnade by Gianlorenzo Bernini, 1656–67

215. The Piazza Colonnade, and the city viewed from S. Peter's nave roof

216. Plan of church and piazza colonnade

sculptural in its handling of masses but the Baroque architect displayed an exuberance and sensuality not to be seen in Renaissance work. Like Michelangelo, his greatest and most important work was at *S. Peter's*, where he became architect in 1629. After his work on the *baldacchino* and some figure sculpture, he designed the *piazza* and *colonnade* in front of the basilica. The problems—aesthetic, practical and liturgical—were immense and only a man of Bernini's stature and artistic authority could have solved them. His vast elliptical colonnades are symbolic of S. Peter's, the Mother Church of Christendom, embracing the world. Their western ends are joined to the basilica façade by two long corridors. The piazza successfully provides space for accommodating the vast crowds who came to see and hear the Pope give his blessing to the city and the world from the façade loggia. Architecturally, these colonnades made history. Unlike the many examples from Ancient Rome, they are not arcades, but the continuous Ionic entablature rests immediately upon the Doric/Tuscan columns which stand four deep, 60 feet high, surmounted by a procession of saints extending outwards from the façade parapet of S. Peter's all round the piazza. The fame of these colonnades spread all over Europe and they were widely emulated for over 200 years in places as far apart as England and Russia (214, 215, 216). The ceremonial entrance staircase, the *Scala Regia*, was adapted and redesigned by Bernini so successfully that it became one of his masterpieces. The existing walls made a narrow dark well but, by his articulation of the walls and adjustment of the stair flights, he gave the impression of greater width. The Baroque handling of light and the elaborate coffered vault above combine to make this one of the great staircases of the world.

At the age of 60 Bernini built *S. Andrea al Quirinale* in *Rome*. On centralised plan in oval form (218), it became one of the prototypes for Baroque churches everywhere. Inside, wall pilasters support an oval entablature and dome. Bernini's handling of the light in this small, perfect interior is masterly as is also his treatment of colour and sculpture. All is dark below with attention drawn to the heavenly dome above with the figure of S. Andrew as a centrepiece in front. The exterior entrance porch shows the powerful vitality of the master in contrast to a severe, monumental façade (219).

Bernini contributed extensively to secular work in *palaces* and in *fountains*. He participated in the work on many palaces, sometimes with others as at *Palazzo Barberini* (from 1629) or, carrying out much of the work himself, as at the *Palazzo Montecitorio* (1650) and the *Palazzo Chigi-Odescalchi* (1664).

Bernini's work as a sculptor is beyond the scope of this book but his contribution to the unique *fountains of Rome* was so large-scale and remarkable that it became an essential feature in architectural town planning, as in the *Piazza Barberini* and the *Piazza Navona*. The *Triton fountain* (1642–3) in the Barberini square shows his breakaway from the Florentine Renaissance tradition into a powerful style, full of movement. In the mid-17th century, the Pope wanted to make the *Piazza Navona*, where his family palace was situated, into the finest square of Rome. An unusual shape due to its development on the exact pattern of the Roman Emperor Diocletian's stadium, S. Agnese was built on one of the long sides and three fountains were equally spaced along the major axis of the piazza. Bernini designed two of these, the Moro and the Fiumi. The latter, the *fountain of the rivers*, dates from 1648; it is the perfect centrepiece to the piazza, setting off the church behind, showing it to advantage but not competing for effect. An obelisk rises in the middle from a rocky base on which are the personifications of four rivers. From the water hole underneath emerges, on one side, a lion, on the other, a horse. This fountain sums up Bernini's contribution to sculptural and architectural decoration. It is a living, pulsing composition, the flowing water used as an integral part of the design to give vitality to the sculpture. The action is caught at an instant of time but is not static, always about to continue the movement (222).

Francesco Borromini 1599–1667

A contemporary of Bernini, Borromini could not have been a greater contrast. He was a recluse, a neurotic, unhappy man who eventually took his own life. His work was brilliant but totally different

217. Interior, S. Giovanni in Laterano, Francesco Borromini, 1646–9

218. Plan. S. Andrea al Quirinale

219. Entrance porch. S. Andrea al Quirinale. Gianlorenzo Bernini 1658–78

220. S. Ivo alla Sapienza, Francesco Borromini, 1642–60

n approach. Bernini, as the essence of the High Baroque extrovert ideal, was like his colleagues in not challenging the basis of Renaissance thought despite the differences in the Baroque interpretation of it. His architectural style was closely linked to sculpture and to a lesser extent, painting. Borromini, on the other hand, cast aside the conception of a classical architecture tied indissolubly to the proportions of the human body as laid down by Leonardo. He evolved new concepts nearer to engineering thought than sculpture and to Medieval construction rather than Renaissance. The results are, despite this, indisputably Baroque and Borromini. He was an innovator, his work mainly confined to churches in this respect, and the influence of this was lasting and prolonged.

His first church was *S. Carlo alle Quattro Fontane*, built 1638–40 and an immediate sensation. The interior combines three different structural schemes: a Greek cross plan, pendentives supporting an oval dome and Baroque, undulating walls. Instead of the classical method of module design based on the column, he preferred a division into geometric units based on the triangle–a more Medieval concept. Though small, the church appears much larger as its convex and concave walls seem to billow, while the typically Baroque lighting, controlled from one source–the dome–accentuates this. The façade, not built until 1665–8, shows his mature approach, equally revolutionary and equally full of undulating curves.

S. Ivo alla Sapienza, the University Church, begun 1642 (220), forms the termination of a courtyard built earlier by Giacomo della Porta. Borromini continued the arcaded scheme round the façade but added an unusual convex and concave drum, dome and lantern surmounted by a complex diminishing steeple. The interior is revolutionary, bearing little relationship to the exterior. Taking the triangular unit again, the plan is a six-point star. The skilfully handled wall articulation supports an entablature and dome which echoes the plan. The concave sections of the dome are further accentuated by its decoration of diminishing rows of stars.

In 1646 Borromini was asked to restore the Cathedral of Rome, *S. John Lateran*. He was not permitted to re-build the Early Christian basilica so

he performed the difficult task of transforming it into a Baroque church by re-clothing the interior. He encased the columns in twos and faced these pillars with a giant order of pilasters extending the whole height of the church. Between these he set niches containing large Baroque sculptured figures. It is a pity that he was not permitted to carry out his vault design to complete the scheme* (217). At *S. Agnese* in the *Piazza Navona*, he took over completion of the church from Rainaldi and built the façade 1652–66. Once again he created a fine Baroque silhouette and here brought to successful conclusion the ideal of so many architects of the 16th and 17th century: a finely proportioned dome and drum flanked by twin towers. It was a scheme to be repeated again and again all over Europe (222, 225).

Among the other Baroque architects working in Rome at this time most notable were *Pietro da Cortona* (1596–1669) and *Carlo Rainaldi* (1611–91). Da Cortona was perhaps best known for his painting in Rome and Florence but he also worked with Bernini on the Palazzo Barberini and designed a number of churches. Of especial interest amongst these are *S.S. Martina* and *Luca* 1635–50 and *S. Maria della Pace* 1656–7. *Rainaldi* was engaged in several of the most important schemes of the century in Rome. He worked on S. Agnese before Borromini, he built *S. Maria Campitelli* 1663–7 and added the façade to Maderna's *S. Andrea della Valle* 1661–5. The most extensive of his works was in the town planning scheme of the *Piazza del Popolo*, the first Baroque layout for Rome and an early use of the later French development of the *rond-point* idea. The Porta del Popolo is one of the entrance gates of Rome and it was planned that it should lead into a piazza from whence three streets should radiate to different parts of the city. An obelisk stands in the centre of the piazza and facing it there are two island sites between the three roads. Rainaldi planned two symmetrical churches here and, though the sites differ in size, he made the churches as alike as possible from the exterior, giving one (*S. Maria di Montesanto*) an oval dome, on the narrower site and the other (*S. Maria dei Miracoli*) a

* The 16th-century wooden ceiling, gilded and painted, was preserved.

HIGH BAROQUE CHURCHES

221. Façade.
S. Moisè,
Venice,
Tremignan,
1668

222. S. Agnese in Piazza Navona,
Rome, 1652–66, Borromini.
Foreground: Fontana dei
Fiumi, 1648–51, Bernini

223. S. Maria della Salute,
Venice, 1631–87.
Longhena

224. Plan. S. Maria della Salute

225. Plan. S. Agnese

circular one, on the wider site (226, 227). These domes act as focal centres for the vista of the piazza from the Porta. Rainaldi himself built S. Maria dei Miracoli 1675–9 and started S. Maria di Montesanto in 1662 to a project suggested by Bernini but the church was completed by Carlo Fontana in 1675. Both have pedimented porticoes and octagonal drums below the domes.

Northern Italy – 17th century

The most outstanding Baroque architecture of this century was in *Turin* and *Venice*. In *Milan*, *Lorenzo Binago's* (1554–1629) *S. Alessandro* was followed by *Francesco Ricchino's* (1583–1658) *S. Giuseppe*. The latter began to break from Renaissance classicism rather as Maderna had done in Rome. His *Palazzo di Brera* of 1651–86 has dignity and a unified design more indicative of his mature work. In *Genoa* the *University* represents the best work of the Early Baroque. By *Bartolomeo Bianco* (1589–1657), it boasts a remarkable staircase. The *New Cathedral* at *Brescia* is an imposing building (210). It was begun in 1604 and built over a long period, the dome not being finally completed till the 1820s. The façade is particularly Baroque as is also the interior with finely drawn Corinthian order and detail. The cathedral makes an effective group with the adjoining 11th century rotunda. A similar interior, equally well lit, is the contemporary *Cathedral of S. Pietro* at *Bologna* (208).

Turin

After Emmanuele Filiberto made his capital here in 1563 the city prospered and for two and a half centuries arts and architecture reflected this importance. Carlo Emmanuele I began to lay out the new city in 1620. The novel idea of planning by streets instead of individual *palazzi* was attempted; the *Piazza San Carlo* and the beginnings of the Via Roma were built by 1638 under the architect *Carlo di Castellamente* (229). The political importance of Turin and its establishment as a capital city serving a large area continued during the 17th and 18th centuries, reaching architectural fruition under the genius of Guarini, Juvara and Vittone.

Guarino Guarini (1624–83) was the principal architect during the 17th century. His work has much in common with that of Borromini in Rome. It is original, unusual and Medieval in inspiration, particularly in its construction based on triangles, though Baroque in clothing. From his sojourn in Turin came the Church of S. Lorenzo, S.S. Sindone and the Palazzo Carignano; differing examples illustrating his versatility and originality. The *Sindone Chapel* in the cathedral was built to house the Holy Shroud. Guarini began work in 1667, taking over from Amadeo di Castellamente. His unique contribution is the dome, made up from 36 arches in triangular pendentive construction. He began the *Church of S. Lorenzo* in 1668, on octagonal plan. Again, the dome is unusual; it has a complex, Medieval structure, carried on pendentives set on the diagonal axes, which transform the octagon into a Greek cross at this level. His *Palazzo Carignano* (232, 234) is entirely Baroque with its undulating, brick façade and central rotunda containing an unusual, oval room on the *piano nobile*.

Venice

Apart from Longhena, there was no great architect here at this time. Typical was Scamozzi's academic Mannerism on the more florid Mannerist approach typified by the façade of *S. Moisé* (221). Baldassare Longhena (1598–1682) was the great man and his masterpiece is S. Maria della Salute. It is interesting to note the high percentage of famous Baroque artists who lived to a great age – Bernini in Rome, Longhena in Venice, Fanzago in Naples, to quote only three. A characteristic of these, as well as many others, was their tremendous energy, zest for life and enthusiasm for their work, which reflects all these characteristics.

The *Church of S. Maria della Salute* has a unique site at the head of the Grand Canal. It was built in thanksgiving for the departure of plague from the city in 1630. Begun in 1631, it was not consecrated till 1687, after the architect's death. Apart from its picturesque exterior and position, this is one of the most interesting and unusual structures of the 17th century, where Longhena provided an alternative Baroque approach from that of Rome. His church is a mixture of themes based on the centrally planned buildings of Ancient Rome (S. Costanza), Byzantine (S. Vitale, Ravenna), Bramante

BAROQUE TOWN PLANNING

228. The Spanish Steps, Rome, 1723–5. Francesco de Sanctis. Leading up to the Church of SS. Trinità dei Monti from the Piazza di Spagna. Fountain the 'Barcaccia', Pietro Bernini, 1628

226. Piazza del Popolo, Rome with 'A' the Church of S. Maria di Montesanto and 'B' S. Maria dei Miracoli, 1662–79, Rainaldi, Fontana and Bernini

227. Plan 'A' S: Maria di Montesanto

229. Piazza San Carlo, Turin, 1638, Carlo di Castellamonte

94

231. Palazzo della Consultà, Rome. Ferdinando Fuga, 1732–7

234. Palazzo Carignano, Turin, Guarino Guarini, 1680

232. Upper floor window, Palazzo Carignano

230. Central doorway, Palazzo della Consultà

233. Palazzo Pesaro, Venice, Baldassare Longhena, 1650–80

(S. Marie Delle Grazie, Milan or Todi) and incorporating the Venetian love of colour inherited from the Palladio School of the region. The plan is octagonal with an ambulatory (224) and the interior is simple and plain, contrasting with the flamboyant exterior; essentially Baroque as in the unusual abutment of the dome in the form of giant scrolls supported on the ambulatory arches (223). Amongst the many other examples of Longhena's work are the *Palazzi Rezzonico* and *Pesaro* (233), the *Cathedral* of *Chioggia* 1624–47, the *Churches* of *S. Maria degli Scalzi* 1656 and the *Ospedaletto* 1670–8. Of dramatic interest is his staircase hall in the Monastery of *S. Giorgio*.

The 18th century

Rome

By 1700 classical architecture was in decline. The source of new interpretations of the Ancient Roman theme which had gushed forth in Italy since 1420 began to dry up; the age of eclecticism set in, to last until modern architecture was created in the 20th century. This did not mean that classical architecture had died, indeed, the theme lasted well into the 19th century and beyond, but it appeared only in guises which had been seen before. These became more varied and numerous, for the 18th century was a time of absorbing interest in the antique world as well as in Renaissance and Baroque developments. With all these versions of the classical theme open to study, the possible permutations and combinations were immense.

Italy had led the world in classical architecture and art since 1420, unchallenged and supreme. Apart from a last flowering of work of quality in Rome, Turin and the South, Italian influence was waning in favour of dominance by French Rococo. Even the origins of classicism were being challenged by the German, the French and the English. Despite last ditch battles by that superb draughtsman and historian Giovanni Piranesi (1720–78) it was generally accepted in the second half of the century that Greece was the originator of classical architecture not Rome. Men of breeding, birth and culture flocked to Italy, Dalmatia and Greece in search of the truth of these origins. The accurate

historical story was at last being evaluated. Architects all over Europe practised the classic mode in every possible interpretation from the Parthenon to Bernini.

The first half of the century in Rome saw an exciting revival with many architects producing varied standards of work. The trends were away from exuberant Baroque to a severe classicism like the monumental façades of *S. John Lateran*, *S. Maria Maggiore* (236, 237) and *S. Croce in Gerusalemme* (235) or to a more light-hearted, delicate Rococo characterised by abandonment of orders and freer elegant decoration as at the *Palazzo della Consulta* (230, 231). Of particular interest in town layout are the Spanish Steps and the Trevi Fountain (228). One of the great Rococo works of Rome, the *Spanish Steps* sweep up the steep hillside from the Piazza di Spagna to *Alessandro Specchi's* elegant church of *S.S. Trinità dei Monti*, in triple ascent and dividing as they go. Banked with flowers at Easter time, here is one of the spectacles of Rome. Apart from its nostalgic associations with coins, the *Trevi Fountain* 1735–72 by *Niccolò Salvi* is a remarkable composition. Basically, the classical palace façade with Roman triumphal arch centrepiece provides a background for a living, moving sculptural drama.

Northern Italy

Venetian churches were Baroque versions of Palladio. One of the best is the *Gesuati* by *Giorgio Massari* (238). Many villas sprang up near the city, varying from small houses to palaces. The most impressive of these is the *Villa Pisani* at *Strà* by *Francesco Preti* 1735–56. This is also Palladian in Baroque clothing.

Turin was the northern centre for great architecture in the first half of the century. Here, *Filippo Juvara* (1678–1736) was the leader, continuing the development of the city and surroundings where Guarini had left off. Juvara was a Sicilian but came to Turin to work for the king. In his 20 years he accomplished a prodigous quantity of work, churches, palaces and whole street layouts in the city itself. His style varied according to the commission and the subject; four examples of his work clearly illustrated this:

7 (b). The Triton Fountain, Piazza Barberini, Rome. Gianlorenzo Bernini, 1642–3 (*see* Page 89)

7 (a). Exterior pulpit, Prato Cathedral. Donatello and Michelozzo, 1434–8

8 (a). Dome and pendentives of S. Lorenzo, Turin. Guarino Guarini, 1668–87 (*see* Page 93)

8 (b). The Trevi Fountain, Rome. Niccolo Salvi, 1735–72 (*see* Page 96)

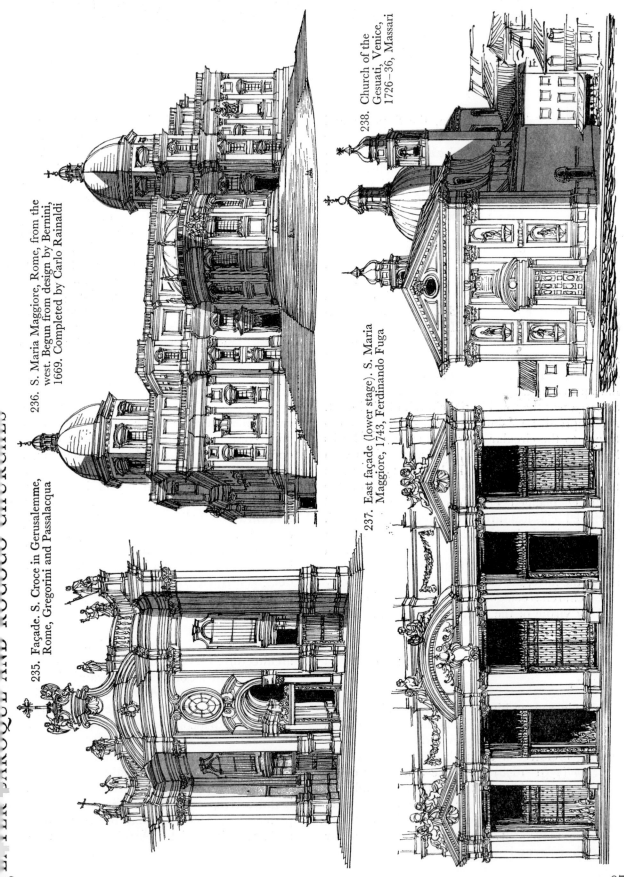

235. Façade, S. Croce in Gerusalemme, Rome, Gregorini and Passalacqua

236. S. Maria Maggiore, Rome, from the west. Begun from design by Bernini, 1669. Completed by Carlo Rainaldi

237. East façade (lower stage). S. Maria Maggiore, 1743, Ferdinando Fuga

238. Church of the Gesuati, Venice, 1726–36, Massari

G

S. Cristina, Palazzo Madama, the Superga and Stupinigi. He added the façade to *S. Cristina* (one of the twin churches in the Piazza San Carlo, built 1639 (229) in 1715–28. This is straightforward Roman Baroque. Also in the city, followed the *Palazzo Madama* in 1718. The façade is richly articulated as befits a town palace and the interior hall and staircase is a masterpiece of elegant design with perfectly handled fenestration and orders (243). In contrast, the hunting lodge at *Stupinigi*, outside the city, is built on large palace scale, very Italian, with different parts grouped round a central Baroque theme which contains a magnificently decorated Rococo hall (239).

Juvara's greatest work is the *Superga*, the finest of all 18th century mountain churches, built on a hill overlooking Turin. It represents the climax of the Baroque era and was its swan song. The Basilica di Superga was the royal burial church of Piedmont. An impressive Corinthian portico provides entrance to the circular church, surmounted by its large drum and dome (which has affinities with S. Peter's) and which is flanked by two western towers (240, 242). Here is the final word on the centrally planned church concept which had intrigued classical architects since Brunelleschi. The interior is large scale, well integrated but simple; the structure is reminiscent of the Pantheon with circular dome rising from the circular drum above the nave, the difference being that the body of the church is octagonal. It is light both in colour and by virtue of the plentiful drum fenestration (241).

Southern Italy and Sicily c. 1590 – c. 1780

Naples

The vigorous architectural movement here of the early 17th century extended to the 18th; the years 1730–60 were particularly fruitful for the arts. The leading architect of the 17th century was *Cosimo Fanzago* (1591–1678) who, like a number of his colleagues, was born in the north but established himself in Naples because of the architectural opportunity of the time. The southern Italian Baroque movement was strongly influenced by Spanish rule and ornament was patterned on

plateresque lines with rich decoration and colou in different marbles. Much of Fanzago's work wa ecclesiastical, his best church being *S. Mari Egiziaca* in Naples, begun 1615, which bears som resemblance to Borromini's S. Agnese in Rome. Hi simple *cloisters* at *S. Martino* are very fine.

18th century architecture in Naples was led b *Luigi Vanvitelli* (1700–73), whose best known wor is the vast *royal palace* at *Caserta* which, like Juvara Superga, was the royal swan song of Baroqu architecture, this time in the south. Built as th Bourbon summer residence, the palace wa designed as the chief feature in the open countrysid to be linked to Naples (16 miles away) by an avenu of trees. The plan is a hollow rectangle; the 850 fee long façade, in an almost uninterrupted horizont: line, still dominates the town of Caserta (245). Th interior is magnificent Baroque in the handling c space and light, especially the monument: ceremonial staircase which ascends from the octa gonal vestibule to another such hall; through i openings can be glimpsed varied changing vista of state rooms. The scenic quality is breathtakin (244). The vast garden layout is modelled o Versailles but is unusually long, extending tw miles in a straight line from the palace via fountain cascades and stairways, rising slowly to culminat in two great fountains on a grand terrace below long cascade. The water for this came via the aque duct, constructed by Vanvitelli, from the mour tains twenty miles away.

Apulia

This area was earlier famed for its Norma architecture. Once again, in the 17th century, : became a district of great and beautiful building almost as if the 500 years in between had neve been. Like the Norman work the Baroque style her was subject to a complex mixture of influences du to racial mingling, also foreign dominance, th time, Spanish. Because of its remoteness from Rom and other centres of the Renaissance arts, the ne\ learning had been slow to percolate through. Whe it did arrive, it was to mingle with the Spanis plateresque, Medieval and Byzantine traditior and Neapolitan gaiety. This all fused into a remark ably stable theme in which the rich decoration wa

239. Royal Hunting Lodge at Stupinigi, 1729–33

240. Plan. Superga

241. Interior of dome, Superga

242. The Basilica di Superga, 1717–31

244. Royal Palace, Caserta (near Naples), begun 1752, Vanvitelli, the staircase

245. Caserta, the façade

243. Staircase hall, Palazzo Madama, Turin, 1718–21, Juvara

f a purely surface character, superimposed on the
Baroque classicism beneath. The small town of
Lecce is the centre of this work and still preserves
many examples, built over a long period in the 17th
and 18th centuries by different architects. Outstanding are the *Church of S. Croce* (246), the
cathedral façade (248) and the adjacent *Seminario*
(249).

Sicily

From about 1600 onwards, Sicilian architecture
was carried out by Sicilians (previously the designs
were more often by architects from the mainland).
Unfortunately most of the 17th century work was
lost in the earthquakes of 1693 which swept the
eastern part of the island; Messina, rebuilt in
Baroque style in the 18th century was destroyed
yet again in 1908. *Palermo* is the only large town to
possess much 17th century work. More like 16th
century style from north Italy, the *Quattro Conti*—
the buildings sited on the crossroads of two of the
main streets—are based on the Quattro Fontane
in Rome (page 91). The *Arsenal* is another example
of such work.

The High Baroque style came to Sicily in the 18th
century, in the works of such architects as *Paolo*
(1633–1714) and *Giacomo Amato* (1643–1732),
Pompeo Picherali (1668–1746) and *Giovanni
Vaccarini* (1702–68). The façade of the *Cathedral
in Syracuse* (247) is a typical work of high quality,
considerably different from that to be seen in Lecce.
This cathedral, it will be remembered, is unusual
in incorporating a Greek temple, the columns still
visible in the aisle walls (page 13). *Vaccarini* was
the architect who replanned *Catania* after the 1693
earthquake, being responsible for the fine buildings
of the cathedral, the churches of S. Chiara,
S. Placido and S. Agata, as well as the Palazzo
Municipale. These are all very Sicilian, totally in
contrast to Lecce Baroque, and nearer to North
Italian Rococo.

Other notable buildings of the period

Cathedral of Palermo, Sicily: cupola, Fuga, 1780s.
Cappella del Crocifisso in Monreale Cathedral,
Sicily, Italia, 1688–92.

Cappella Paolina in S. Maria Maggiore, Rome,
Ponzio, 1611.
Chiesa del Carmine, Turin, Juvara, 1732.
Chiesa dell'Annunziata, Naples, Vanvitelli, 1761–82.
Chiesa della Pietà, Palermo, Sicily, Amato, 1689–
1723.
Chiesa del Rosario, Lecce, Zimbalo, 1691.
Church of S. Anna, Palermo, Amico, 1736.
Church of S. Biagio in Campitelli, Rome, Carlo
Fontana, 1665.
Church of S. Carlo all'Arena, Naples, Fra Nuvolo,
1631.
Church of S. Filippo, Turin, begun Guarini 1679,
continued Juvara.
Church of S. Gaetono, Florence, Silvani, early 17th
century.
Mountain pilgrimage church of S. Madonna di S.
Luca, near Bologna, Dotti, 1723–57.
Church of S. Maria dei Setti Dolori, Rome, Borro-
mini, 1650–60.
Church of S. Maria della Sanità, Naples, Fra Nuvolo,
1602.
Church of S.S. Nicola e Cataldo, Lecce, Cino, 1716.
Church of S.S. Vincenzo ed Anastasio, Rome, Longhi,
1646–50.
Collegio dei Nobili (now Academy of Science and Art
Gallery), Turin, Guarini, 1678.
Galleria Borghese, Pincio, Rome, Vansanzio, 1613–
1615.
Oratory of S. Filippo Neri, Rome, Borromini, 1637–
1640.
Palazzo Bonagia, near Palermo, Giganti, 1731–87.
Palazzo Falconieri, Rome, Borromini, *c.* 1640.
Palazzo Grassi, Venice, Massari, 18th century.
Palazzo Laterano, Rome, Domenico Fontana, 1586.
Palazzo Marescotti, Rome, della Porta, late 16th
century.
Palazzo Mattei, Rome, Carlo Maderna, 1598–1618.
Palazzo Pamphili, Rome, Borromini, 1647.
Palazzo Quirinale, Rome, enlarged and altered from
1615, Ponzio.
Palazzo Serra Cassano, Naples, Sanfelici, 1725–6.
Prefettura, Lecce, Zimbalo, 1659–95.
Villa Palagonia, near Palermo, Napoli, 1715.

246. Façade. Church of S. Croce, Lecce.
Lower Part 1582, Gabrieli Riccardi.
Upper part 1624, Cesare Penna

247. Façade. Cathedral of Syracuse,
1728–54. Andrea Palma

248. Gable of façade. Lecce Cathedral,
1659–82, Giuseppe Zimbalo

249. Façade. Lecce
Seminario,
1694–1709,
Giuseppe Cino

780 to the Present Day

CHAPTER 9

Eclecticism 1780–1920

THROUGHOUT Europe all the architecture till 900 was based on what had gone before. It can be said that this was also true of buildings erected since 1450 but designers of the Renaissance, Baroque and Rococo eras, though inspired by earlier work, brought to their interpretation something new and personal. We can see this in the different viewpoints on the classical theme expressed by such men as Brunelleschi, Bramante, Michelangelo, Bernini, all of whom took their ideas from Ancient Rome but all impressed upon these themes their own, original conceptions, so creating something new.

The 19th century was not like this. In Europe, in general, from about 1780 until the emergence of modern architectural thought just after the end of the First World War, all architecture was unoriginal in conception and treatment. Also, unfortunately, the copy was inferior to the original. This is not to say that good designs were not made or good quality architecture built. It was simply the mixture as before but a re-interpretation of all previous styles from Byzantine and Romanesque to 18th century Rococo. 19th century architects tried it all. Romanesque, Byzantine and Gothic styles were reserved chiefly for churches, schools, houses and universities, with the classical themes applied to civic building and town layouts.

Italy, due no doubt to her strong classical tradition extending almost unbroken from the Roman Empire, was different from other European countries in her eclectic approach. Italian architects used only classical models with a hint of Byzantine decoration or treatment. Any Gothic or Romanesque work in Italy is a repair or restoration of a Medieval building or was built by a foreign architect. *Florence Cathedral* façade is a notable

example of the former and the English architect *G. E. Street* of the latter in his churches in *Rome*: All Saints', constructed for the English community and St. Paul's for the American. Indeed, St. Paul's Church, 1873–6, in the Via Nazionale reminds one of London churches of the period with its red and white polychrome treatment and tall bell-tower. Of especial interest inside are the apse mosaics by *Burne-Jones*, glowing with colour and gold, depicting Christ in Majesty. Both church and decoration are high quality English exports.

Italian architects and artists had led Europe in new movements and ideas as well as quality of craftsmanship since 1450. By 1780 this lead had disappeared. People still came to Italy in large numbers, not to study the works of contemporary architects but to see the creations of the past. Architectural development was in the doldrums everywhere between 1790–1805 due to the Napoleonic Wars, with an exception in the case of England which was less closely involved. After this, Napoleon himself instigated many new building schemes in France and in occupied countries like Italy. The lead had passed to France and later in the century to Germany and England. Italian architects, though producing work comparable to many architects of other nations, no longer pointed the way. Much of the architecture in Italy of the 19th century in general has been deprecated more by the Italians than by others for, after so glorious a tradition over so many centuries, it was an anticlimax to be merely following the foreign lead. Several of the Italian town planning schemes, especially in the first half of the century, have been undervalued and are only now becoming appreciated for their worth. Italian work in the 19th

250. Piazza Vittorio Veneto, Turin, 1818,
Guiseppe Frizzi and Carlo Promis

251. Portico, S. Francesco di Paolo

252. S. Francesco di Paolo, Naples,
1816–24, Pietro Bianchi

century, unlike that in a number of other European countries, is not often in bad taste. It is generally less overdecorated than in England, France or Germany in that period of ostentation of the 1870s and 1880s which followed the Romantic Classicism of the 1820s and 1830s. Italian work of this century is not exciting, it is certainly duller and inferior to that of the preceding centuries but its standard varies from good to adequate: it is rarely bad.

The achievements of the time can be studied simply in the following groups:

1. Town planning and civic layouts.
2. Restoration of Medieval work.
3. Memorials.
4. Iron and glass construction.
5. Art Nouveau.

Town Planning and civic layouts

The outstanding work in this field is in *Turin*, *Trieste* and *Naples* from the first half of the century and in *Rome* from the later years. Of this, the work in *Turin* is both the most extensive and of greatest merit. It continues the 17th and 18th century tradition here of an artistic centre and one noted for its planning by streets and squares and not only of individual buildings (pp. 96, 98). The city centre was expanded along lines similar to the existing work. Due to the city's geographical position and links with France, Turin architecture always had a French flavour. The great squares and wide arcaded streets laid out in the first decades of the 19th century illustrate this French influence. The two chief schemes are the vast *Piazza Vittorio Veneto* (250) which debouches from the arcaded Via Po towards the river, the vista terminated by the *Church of Gran Madre di Dio* (254), built 1818–31 to commemorate the re-establishment of the Savoy monarchy in its capital after the withdrawal of Napoleonic occupation. The Church itself is one of

the many Pantheon inspired examples, not especially noteworthy, but the piazza is well and homogenously designed. On the other side of the city centre the Via Roma divides into the two branches of the *Piazza Carlo Felice* which end in the busy Corso Emmanuele II where the vista is blocked by the immense façade of the *Porta Nuova railway station* (256). This is a scheme of the 1820s and 1830s, again displaying homogeneity, with interesting façades to the buildings in the piazza and a decorative and constructive use of the fashionable materials of iron and glass in the station itself.

The *Trieste* scheme is in the district of the *Canale Grande*, on the waterfront. This is more Italian than the work in Turin though of much the same date. The Canale Grande itself is a rectangular stretch of water extending landwards at right angles to the harbour, on each side of which are palaces and houses with the terminal vista occupied by the *Church of S. Antonio di Padova*. This church (another Pantheon), standing in the same relative position as the Gran Madre in Turin, is more accomplished in design and has a better situation (255). Along the waterfront on either side of the Canale are palaces, such as the Carciotti, which are of fine standard for 19th century work.

The *Church of S. Francesco di Paolo* in *Naples* is a highly eclectic composition with its centrepiece based on the Pantheon and its colonnade on Bernini's S. Peter's (251, 252). It is very successful, an impressive, large-scale design, only marred by the sea of cars parked over the whole piazza in front of the church. Nearby, the enlarged and renovated *Royal Palace* stretches its immense façade high above the quay. Also eclectic, this is equally successful in its repetitive design (253). Not far away is the Romantic Classical *San Carlo Opera House* which has an elegant Ionic colonnaded upper storey above the rusticated and Greek panelled

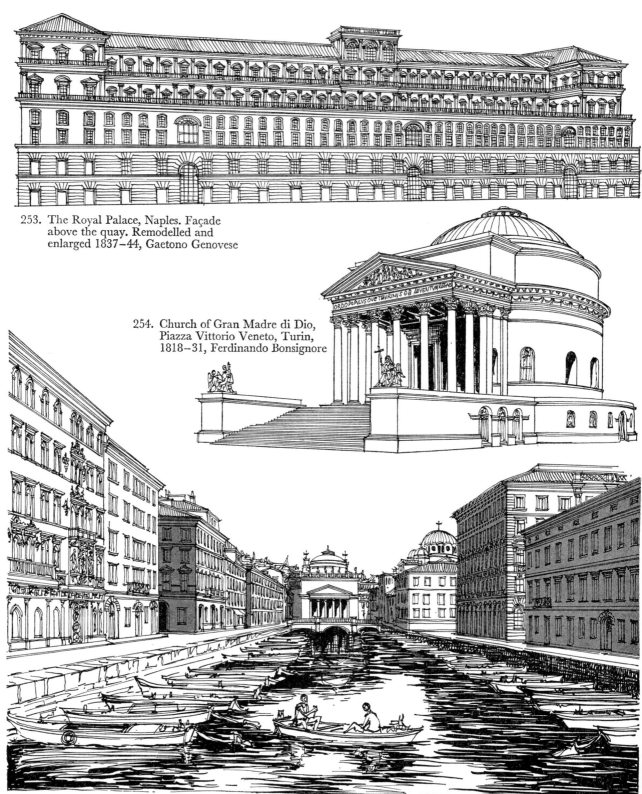

253. The Royal Palace, Naples. Façade
above the quay. Remodelled and
enlarged 1837–44, Gaetono Genovese

254. Church of Gran Madre di Dio,
Piazza Vittorio Veneto, Turin,
1818–31, Ferdinando Bonsignore

255. Canale Grande layout with Church
of Antonio di Padova at end of vista,
Trieste, 1826–49, Peter von Nobile

lower level. Built in 1810 by *Niccolini*, it has a sumptuous interior.

After the unification of Italy, *Rome* became the capital and from the 1870s onwards the city was expanded and a number of large schemes were initiated. Of the extant buildings of this time, the *Piazza Esedra* is especially impressive. Its sweeping façades curve round in quarters of a circle at the head of the Via Nazionale, set off by the vigorous fountain design in the centre (257). Typical of the large individual buildings are a number in the Via Nazionale itself, such as the Palazzo delle Belle Arti (258, 259) and the Banca d'Italia of 1885–1904.

Medieval restoration and completion

The Italians, like other European nations, completed and restored a number of great Medieval buildings in the 19th century. Most of these were ecclesiastical and, as elsewhere, great care was taken to create facsimiles of the Medieval craftsmanship of design. *Milan Cathedral* façade was finally completed at the beginning of the century in a mixture of classicism and northern Gothic, the doorways in particular being straightforwardly classical with typical 19th century sculpture. In *Florence*, the façade was added to the *Church of S. Croce* 1857–63 by *Niccolò Matas* while at the *Cathedral* the façade was finally completed in 1887. The work was carefully carried out by *Emilio de Fabris* in order to match the existing Medieval marble veneers and design. Despite this it still lacks the full-blooded Gothic approach more to be seen in Street's S. Paul's American Church in Rome.

Memorials

All over Europe, especially in the latter years of the century, this was the age of memorials, to individuals, to events, to causes. Italy was no exception, her sculpture was as dramatic and sentimental as in other countries but invariably it was capably executed with the age-old sensitivity of the Italian craftsman to his marble and bronze. The most famous of all memorials in Italy is the immense white marble structure in the Piazza Venezia in *Rome*, to *King Victor Emmanuel II*. Called *La Torta Nuziale* (wedding cake) by the Romans, it is now, like the Albert Memorial in London, regarded as an integral part of the city life, still scorned by the intelligentsia but a magnet for tourists of all nations, Italians included. It represents the epitome of the 1880s in all European nations, large scale, producing a visual dramatic impact, imperial, richly ornamented, magnificently carried out and considerably larger than life size, not only in a literal but a metaphorical sense. The Roman example catches the eye more than its English equivalent because of its dazzling white marble shining in the Italian sunshine. It is clean, sparkling, immense. In classical dress with sculpture in white marble and bronze, it is the exact Italian equivalent to the English Albert Memorial, dedicated to King and Empire, advocating sacrifice and sentiment, viewed through slightly rose-tinted spectacles. It is extremely probable that, as tastes and fashions change inexorably with the passing of time, it will acquire within the next 20 years, like the Albert Memorial and St. Pancras Station have done, first respectability and then admiration (260, 261).

On the summit of the Janiculum Hill in Rome, high above S. Peter's and the Tiber is an equestrian monument to another hero of the Risorgimento, *Guiseppe Garibaldi* erected in 1895 to the design of *Gallori*. There are the usual late 19th century dramatic groups on each of the four sides of the pedestal while, less commonly, are busts of the '1000' bordering the long approach advances up the hill.

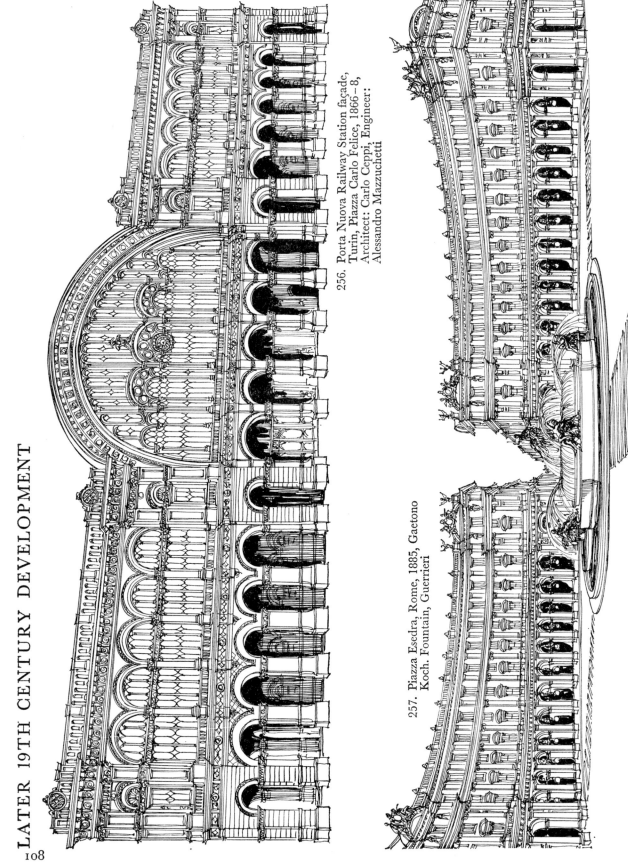

256. Porta Nuova Railway Station façade, Turin, Piazza Carlo Felice, 1866–8, Architect: Carlo Ceppi, Engineer: Alessandro Mazzuchetti

257. Piazza Esedra, Rome, 1885, Gaetono Koch. Fountain, Guerrieri

on and Glass

The advances in building construction and technique made possible by the developments in iron, steel and glass provide the one exception to the eclecticism of the period. Here is one characteristic that is quite new but it was commonly employed in traditional artistic designs. These new techniques made it easier to build large scale structures which had not been seen hitherto. England, which in the 18th century had been the first country to experience the industrial revolution, naturally became the first also to develop the new media. The Ironbridge at Coalbrookdale was the first in the world, built in 1779. The age of the great engineers in England—Telford, Rennie, Stephenson, Brunel—was 1820–50. By the 1870s all Western Europe was using the new methods, building bridges, railway stations, covered arcades and markets on Crystal Palace lines (though not as pre-fabricated structures). As France of this time is famed for its Eiffel Tower, so Italy is known for the arcade in *Milan* called, inevitably, the *Galleria Vittorio Emmanuele II*. It is a tremendous structure on cruciform plan extending from the Piazza del Duomo to the Piazza della Scala behind. Like a cathedral there is a centrepiece over the crossing and the entrance resembles a tremendous triumphal arch (263). Within, under the glass and metal roof are exclusive shops and cafés. The decoration and sculpture is of the period, mostly in iron, painted and still in good, of restored condition (262, 264). Today the arcade still fulfils its original function, it is the central meeting place of life in Milan, just as the Roman Forum was in its day, protecting the people from rain and sunshine alike. There are other galleries in different towns, of much the same date, although less impressive. The best known are in *Genoa* and *Naples*. Like the rest of Europe, Italy produced vast *railway station* façades for its large towns, a number of which still exist. Of the iron and glass type: the one at Turin (page 105) is a good example (256).

Art Nouveau

The expression 'Art Nouveau' has been used here because it is the English one for this unusual, brief episode in the history of art and architecture. The English have here, of course, adopted the French word* as they did with Renaissance and Baroque. Other nations have different expressions to describe what almost defies description, so varied is it in national interpretation and so ephemeral in its lasting qualities. The Italians called it '*lo stile floreale*' or, alternatively, '*lo stile Liberty*', not, as one might imagine at first sight, because it had anything to do with freedom, but after the famous London store in Regent Street, which, at the time, displayed fabrics patterned on these lines. For, although Art Nouveau was an international movement, it was not outstandingly architectural but decorative, its manifestations were primarily in textiles, coloured glass, metalwork and painting. There was very little Art Nouveau architecture in England, still less in the USA. The movement began in Belgium, then became popular in France, Germany, Italy and Spain though it took very different forms in these countries. Architecturally one of its chief features is in decoration and structural form in iron and glass, stemming originally from such constructions as the Eiffel Tower and the Galleria in Milan. Developed by men such as Victor Horta in Brussels in the 1890s, it spread to other countries, lasting a very short time and by 1910 had almost vanished leaving little trace and even less influence on later work. Yet, despite its ephemeral appearance, Art Nouveau is noteworthy as the first original style to

* Though the French themselves often refer to it as the 'modern style'.

258. Palazzo delle Belle Arti, 1882, Pio Piacentini

260. Bronze equestrian statue of Victor Emmanuel II. Detail of Monument

259. Detail, Palazzo delle Belle Arti

261. Monument to Victor Emmanuel II, 1885–1911. Many architects, including Sacconi, Koch, Piacentini, Manfredi and Brasini

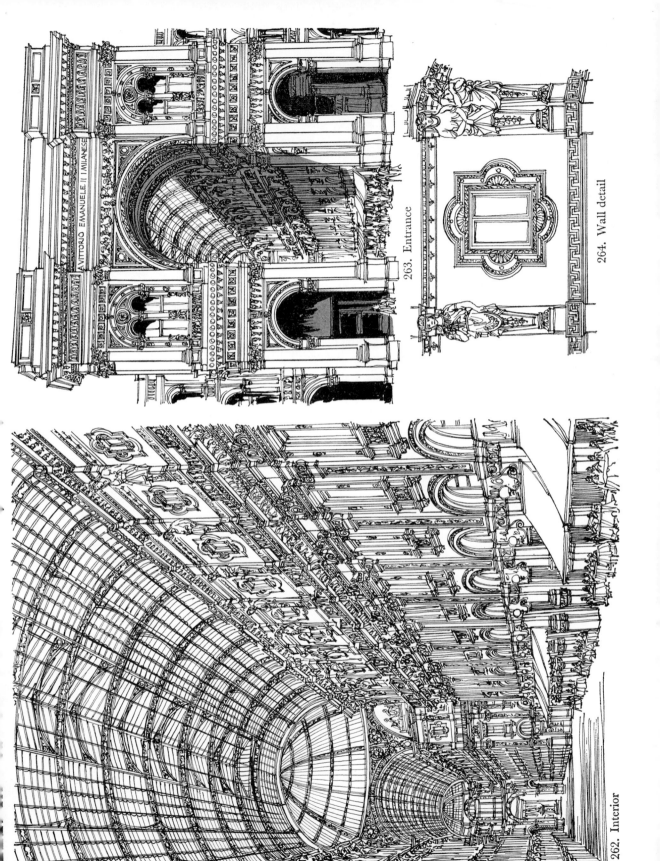

263. Entrance

264. Wall detail

262. Interior

A VITTORIO EMANUELE II I MILANESI

III

ART NOUVEAU

265. Casa Castiglione, 47 Corso Venezia,
Milan, 1903, Giuseppe Sommaruga

appear—that is not Gothic or Classical—for hundreds of years in Europe and, as such, was the first breakaway which led eventually to modern architecture. It must be stressed though, that the style of Art Nouveau itself has no connection with modern development in architectural form.

Art Nouveau in Italy dates chiefly from the first decade of the 20th century. Its architectural exponents included *Basile*, *D'Aronco* known for his exhibition buildings in north Italy, *Cattaneo* who built a hotel in Milan in the style and *Sommaruga* whose large, extrovert block of flats still exists in the Corso Venezia in *Milan* (265). This is typical of the more extravagant Italian version of the theme with its bellicose putti hanging on to the window frames in uncomfortable attitudes and the 'hewn out of the living rock' quality of the tower storey—a kind of

Art Nouveau rustication. A more elegant example also in Milan, is the insurance building in the Piazza dei Liberty (now restored). The ground floor is modernised but above the *putti* are here more comfortably and happily perched on their fenestration

Other notable buildings of the period

Church of S. Massimo, Turin, Sada, 1845–54.
La Scala Opera House, Milan, exterior 1776–8 but interior 1830 by Sanguirico, also the building opposite, 1830–45.
Palazzo Lucini, Via Monti, Milan, Crivelli, 1831.
Palazzo Margherita (now American Embassy), Via Vittorio, Rome, Koch, 1886–90.
Piazza della Repubblica, Florence, Poggi, 1887–95.

920 to the Present Day

ODERN architecture, by which term is meant
uilding of the 20th century which does not derive
om classical and Medieval origins, developed in
ree principal stages. These comprise the work of
e early years of the century until the outbreak of
e First World War (Chapter 9), the inter-war
ears and the post war period. In some countries
Europe the eclectic approach of the 19th century
ntinued until at least 1950. The chief of these was
ngland, where a classical design for a public
uilding was considered the only respectable
eme: the leading exponent here was Sir Edwin
utyens. In ecclesiastical work, Sir Giles Gilbert
cott followed traditional Gothic patterns. Most of
e rest of Western Europe pursued a mixed course.
Iodern work, on the lines of simple, basic, func-
onal and often stark buildings, was erected in
ermany, the Low Countries, France, Italy and
witzerland but, even here, it was until about 1950
e minority of building work, although it enjoyed
e attention and participation of the outstanding
rchitects of these countries. Political and economic
ctors, in the years 1920–39, had tremendous
npact. In Germany, for instance, the Bauhaus
leas put forward by Walter Gropius and his col-
agues were cut short by Hitler's rise to power. It
 a feature of authoritarian governments, im-
aterial whether fascist or communist, that control
the arts for propaganda purposes is absolute and
is control is invariably reactionary. The result in
ermany was the emigration of her most original
inking architects (as well as scientists, doctors,
c.) first to England and France, later to the USA.
Italy, despite her fascist régime of the time,
ffered, in the arts at least, less severely. Mussolini
d grand ideas of a new Roman Empire and so

favoured the classical ideal. His chosen architects,
therefore, carried out imperial schemes but they
were never as restricted as in Germany. Italy was a
contributor to early modern architecture, beginning in the First World War with Sant'Elia and
continuing with such men as Terragni, Pagano,
Faludi (273), Ponti and others.

Antonio Sant'Elia (1880–1916) was born in Como.
He was a remarkable visionary of future architecture, devising designs of modern cities far in advance of his time. He developed socialistic themes
for ideal societies which were revolutionary at the
time he put them forward. Tragically, his talents
were cut short in 1916 when he was killed in action
and all we have of his ideas are drawings and designs
which, nevertheless, strongly influenced later work.

In the early 1920s it was *Giuseppe Terragni* (1904–
1943) who led Italy's modern school of thought.
Terragni was enabled to work long enough to
produce a number of interesting buildings which
had an international effect on the modern scene
but his life too was cut short, this time in the Second
World War. His working years were few, lasting
from his graduation from the Milan Polytechnic
in 1926 till his call-up in 1939. In 1926 he helped to
found the *gruppo sette*, seven architects who joined
the '*Movimento Italiano per l'Architettura Razionale*'.
They stood for a new basic architectural theme,
searching for clarity, order and honesty in use of
materials and abhorring the revivalism of bygone
styles. These men were all young and were inspired
by Gropius' Bauhaus, his colleagues Mies van der
Rohe and Peter Behrens, also the work of men like
Frank Lloyd Wright in the USA. Terragni's outstanding works were the *Casa del Fascio* in *Como*, his
apartment blocks in *Como* (268) and the *Casa Rustici*

H

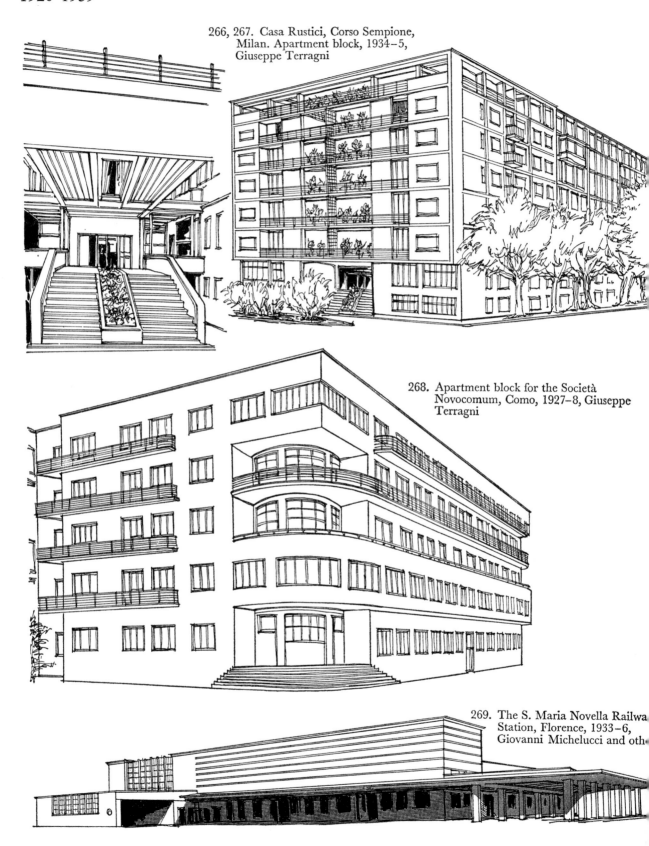

266, 267. Casa Rustici, Corso Sempione, Milan. Apartment block, 1934–5, Giuseppe Terragni

268. Apartment block for the Società Novocomum, Como, 1927–8, Giuseppe Terragni

269. The S. Maria Novella Railway Station, Florence, 1933–6, Giovanni Michelucci and oth

in *Milan* (266, 267), they formed landmarks in the modern world, not only affecting work in Italy but in Europe. Despite his limited time for architectural work he created a permanent effect in establishing the pattern of modern building–plain, severe, uncompromising and functional.

Giuseppe Pagano (1896–1945) also fought and died in the Second World War. He was of Austro-Hungarian parentage, being born Pogatschnig, in Parenzo (now Poreč) and changed his name in 1915. He qualified in 1924 in Turin and became known partly for his writing and partly for his architectural work such as the *Palazzo degli Uffici Gualino* in *Turin* (1928–9) and his *Istituto Fisico* (Department of Physics Building) at the *University of Rome* (272). The *Città Universitaria* here is a large campus laid out in the 1930s. The entrance is a plain rectangular block type propylaeum of white stone and most of the faculty buildings, like the Physics one, are in red brick. The whole scheme is plain and functional but of good design and construction. Also of interest is the *library*, forming the end of the vista, built *c.*1935 by *Ridolfo* (274). Pagano worked on other university schemes notably the *Università Commerciale Bocconi* at *Milan* (1938–41). This is even plainer and more functionalist.

Many Italian architects of the 1930s have proved exceptionally versatile and, though building in severe block form then, have adapted themselves in the post-war period to the more varied modern approach. Among such architects can be numbered *Giovanni Michelucci* (b.1891) who designed the *S. Maria Novella Railway Station* in *Florence* in 1933–6 (269) then carried on to the *Savings Bank* in *Florence* 1957–8 (285) and to *churches* of a more original type such as *S. Giovanni* near *Florence* in 1961. *Eugenio Montuori* (b.1907) was another such man, creating under Mussolini the *Central Railway Station* in *Milan* (275), and continuing, with others, to the successful *Termini Station* in *Rome*, of international fame, in 1951 (277). *Gio Ponti* (b.1891) renowned for the *Pirelli Tower* (284) and one of Italy's best known architects today was also a notable architect in the 1930s, though he did not join with *gruppo sette* in its revolt against revivalism and objections to ornamental decoration.

The leading architect of the traditional classical school was *Marcello Piacentini* (b.1881), whose work, despite its eclecticism, possessed vision and vitality. In *Bergamo* he built the new town layout at the foot of the Medieval hill city–the *Città Bassa*–in 1922–4. He supported fascism and so became the natural selection as principal architect for the Mussolini administration. In the early years of his government Mussolini gave favourable support to modern work but, as his alliance with Hitler grew stronger, the German reactionary attitude to the arts became paramount. Piacentini, under these conditions, was responsible for much of Mussolini's vast project for a new capital outside the city, the '*Terza Roma*', and built a number of new towns south of Rome. Most of this was badly damaged in the Second World War. Still extant, and typical of how Piacentini's traditionalism differs from its English, German and French counterparts in its more modern and lively approach, is his completion of the *Via Roma* in *Turin* between the Piazza San Carlo and the Piazza Carlo Felice (271). This continues the 18th and 19th century scheme for the thoroughfare in a classical, dignified manner, but very much in 20th century dress.

Architecture since 1950

It is a fact, lamented by many cultured people interested in architecture, that buildings erected since the Second World War tend to a sameness of design, materials and handling whether in New York or Tokyo, Berlin or Athens. In Italy too, a large proportion of modern work has its counterparts all over the world: blocks of flats, office towers, university campuses. At the same time, it is also true that Italy has been the most influential and

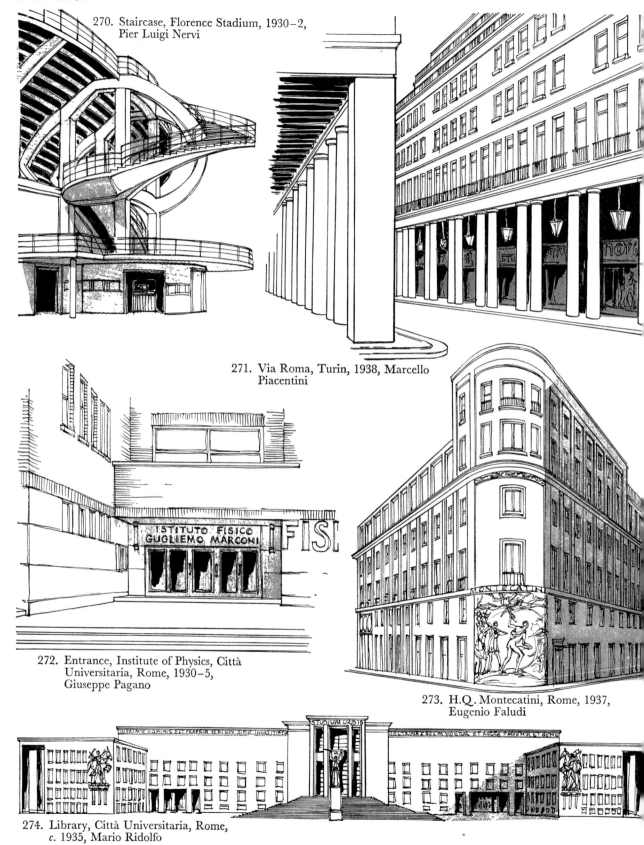

270. Staircase, Florence Stadium, 1930–2,
Pier Luigi Nervi

271. Via Roma, Turin, 1938, Marcello
Piacentini

272. Entrance, Institute of Physics, Città
Universitaria, Rome, 1930–5,
Giuseppe Pagano

273. H.Q. Montecatini, Rome, 1937,
Eugenio Faludi

274. Library, Città Universitaria, Rome,
c. 1935, Mario Ridolfo

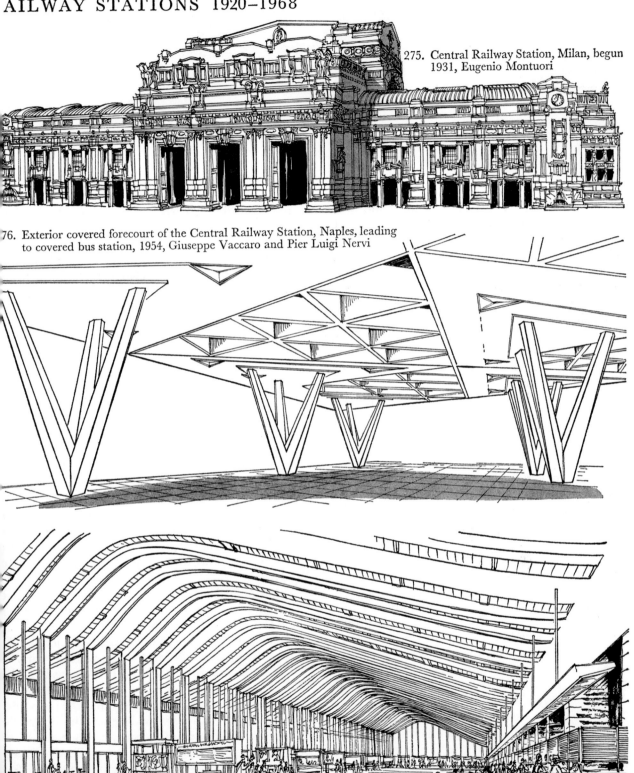

275. Central Railway Station, Milan, begun 1931, Eugenio Montuori

76. Exterior covered forecourt of the Central Railway Station, Naples, leading to covered bus station, 1954, Giuseppe Vaccaro and Pier Luigi Nervi

277. Central Railway Station 'Termini', Rome, 1947–51. Piazza dei Cinquecento, Eugenio Montuori also Calini, Castellazzi, Fatigati, Pintonello, Vitellozzi

leading spirit in the better quality and more original design seen in recent architecture. The USA still keeps its place here as does also Scandinavia but, in Western Europe in general, Italian achievement is significant. Because of this, there is a great interest in Italian modern architecture, in England as elsewhere, and the number of books published in recent years here, devoted entirely to Italian work of the 1950s and 1960s bear testimony to this (see bibliography).

Just after the Second World War ended the need for reconstruction in Italy (as in Germany) was vital and there, as in a number of other European countries, a quantity of buildings were erected of functional type, very much on pre-war designs, not very well constructed, carelessly thought out, and these are beginning to show themselves as the city slums of tomorrow. However, in the 1950s, this was realised and action taken. Both established pre-war architects and younger men, newly qualified, turned to the attempt to improve building standards and design. In many instances they achieved remarkable success. The process still continues and work of the 1960s is steadfastly improving on the previous decade.

The Italian contribution to originality and interest, the two qualities so lacking in the vast proportion of modern architecture all over the world, is in three fields. The quality of material and decoration seen in traditional Italian craftsmanship now modified to unit and mass production methods using coloured marbles, granite and mosaic. Secondly, the tremendous variety of design in shapes and colour. The shapes themselves show a far greater use of curves in both linear and three-dimensional form than are seen in England, for instance, where rectangularity is still the monotonous mode. Due to the climate, bright colours are more necessary and also show to greater advantage. Thirdly, and partly the reason for the ability to use curves on inexpensive buildings, is the concentra-

tion by Italian architects since 1950 on the development of concrete. Partly for economic reasons, this has been preferred to development in steel but the results have produced a greater variety in design. The over-emphasis on steel gives rectangular tower blocks as in the USA, England, Germany. The derivations from concrete have produced an infinite range of self-supporting roofs, vaults and shell coverings which can be seen all over the country in buildings for different functions, from technical colleges to sports halls and offices.

From the quantity of examples available, the illustrations for this chapter have been chosen to show this Italian versatility in shape and material and also how they differ in this respect from their English counterparts. Apartment blocks, private houses and civic work in banks and insurance offices have been largely omitted because it is in these fields that Italian work is similar to that existing in England. Most of the more original architecture is in churches, hotels, office blocks and semi-engineering structures like railway stations, stadia and road and bridge building (276, 281, 282, 283, 285).

Pier Luigi Nervi (b.1891), the great engineer and builder, is the most important figure in Italian development of reinforced concrete. Born at Sondrio, graduating at Bologna in engineering, he established a reputation for this work as early as 1930 in his stadium in Florence. Here, as in all his later works, he has followed his own precepts with astonishing success. He believes that the purpose of architecture is still to provide good building for the user or inhabitant and, at the same time, to act, by its aesthetic qualities as a quiet but effective educational influence. Both these factors have too often been forgotten by crusaders of modern architecture, especially the later 'Brutalists'. Nervi's structures are functional without doubt but, unlike the 'functionalism' of the inter-war years, they are never boring to the eye or unpleasing to the human

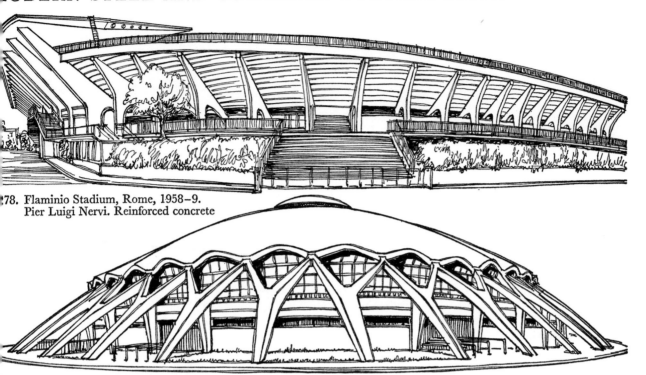

278. Flaminio Stadium, Rome, 1958–9.
Pier Luigi Nervi. Reinforced concrete

279. Palazzetto dello Sport, Rome, 1957,
Annibale Vitellozzi and Pier Luigi
Nervi. Reinforced concrete

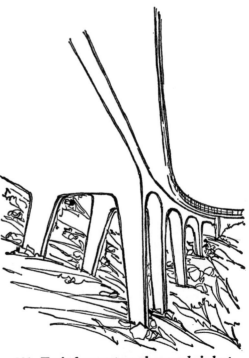

281. Typical concrete modern road viaduct,
southern Italy, 1956, Maresca and
Bellante

280. Palace of Labour, Turin, 1960–1, Pier
Luigi Nervi. Steel and reinforced
concrete

spirit and they always excite admiration and interest. Almost all Nervi's work is in reinforced concrete, adopted in the first place for its cheapness but, unlike so much concrete work in the world, it is not shabby or sordid. The sweeping curves maintain interest and give a chiarascuro at once uplifting and satisfying while maintaining structural stability.

The *stadium* in *Florence* was built 1930-2 (270) and immediately excited curiosity, admiration and controversy from architects all over the world. It illustrates convincingly the immense possibilities of this material. In 1935 Nervi designed a concrete roofed hangar from which a number of examples were constructed between 1936 and 1941, notably at *Orvieto* and *Ortebello*. After the war he continued his experimental studies in roofing and vaulting in concrete producing, among other works, his great masterpiece, the great hall of the *Exhibition Building* at *Turin* (1948-9), widely acclaimed as the most magnificent exhibition hall since the Crystal Palace. Nervi created here a tremendous vaulted but lightweight structure made up of undulating, prefabricated concrete units comprising several halls. The result is a vast and useful exhibition scheme and it possesses an internal ceiling of beauty and interest. Other projects followed; the hall at the *Lido di Roma* (Ostia), at *Chianciano Terme*, the three great structures for the Olympic Games in *Rome:* the *Stadium* (278), the *Palazzo* and the smaller *Palazzetto dello Sport* (279), all in the 1950s. These two sports halls also possess the most original and successful concrete vaulting systems. In 1960, Nervi returned to the Exhibition site in *Turin* to build the *Palace of Labour* for the centenary of Italian Unification in 1861 (280). This vast hall, like the Crystal Palace in London a century before, had to be built quickly and to be suitable for later adaptation for varying purposes. The time factor ruled out the overall use of Nervi's usual material and the hall is partly of steel construction. The columns are made in six vertical, concrete sections (each taking only ten

days to cast) and carrying palm leaf style capita plates resembling modern interpretations of Egyptian lotus capitals from the Nile palaces.

While carrying out these and other enterprises Nervi has ceaselessly applied himself to further research into the uses and limits of his material and into the possibilities of achieving greater success in the creation of rhythmic curves and lines of aesthetic beauty, it is in this latter aim that he goes further than so many of his contemporaries in other countries. His later works, showing something of the success he has won in these objectives, include hi participation as engineering consultant in the *Pirelli Building, Milan* (284), the *railway station* at *Naples*, the *Agnelli Exhibition Hall* at *Turin* and, outside Italy but of especial originality and interest, the *UNESCO Building* and the *Centre National des Industries* in *Paris*.

Mention must be made of important work no illustrated here or yet referred to which should include the contribution in patronage of the *Olivetti Co.* with its offices in Milan (1954 Bernasconi, Fiocchi and Nizzoli), the main plan at Ivrea (1942, Figini and Pollini) and the newe factory at Pozzuoli by Luigi Cosenza and Nervi In *Milan* there is the unusual but now outgrown *Torre Velasca* (1957, Belgiojosa, Peresutti and Rogers), the *Torre Savour* (1956-9, Bega), the *Palazzo del Fuoco* (1959, Minoletti), and the *Faculty of Architecture Buildings* at the *Milan Polytechnic* (Morasutti and Mangiapotti). Among the many new churches, particularly notable are *La Madonna dei Poveri* in Milan (1952-4, Figini and Pollini), the parish church at *Baranzate* (1957-8, Mangiarotti and Morasutti), and the *Redentore*, Turin (Mosso). The last-named is reminiscent of the nearby Sindone Chapel by Guarini (page 93), while the inspiration of the example illustrated, *S. Ildefonso* (288) is its neighbouring S. Maria delle Grazie by Bramante (page 68). Such derivations may be responsible for critical foreign opinion (notably English) condemning Italian modern work as too

BUILDINGS OF THE 1950s

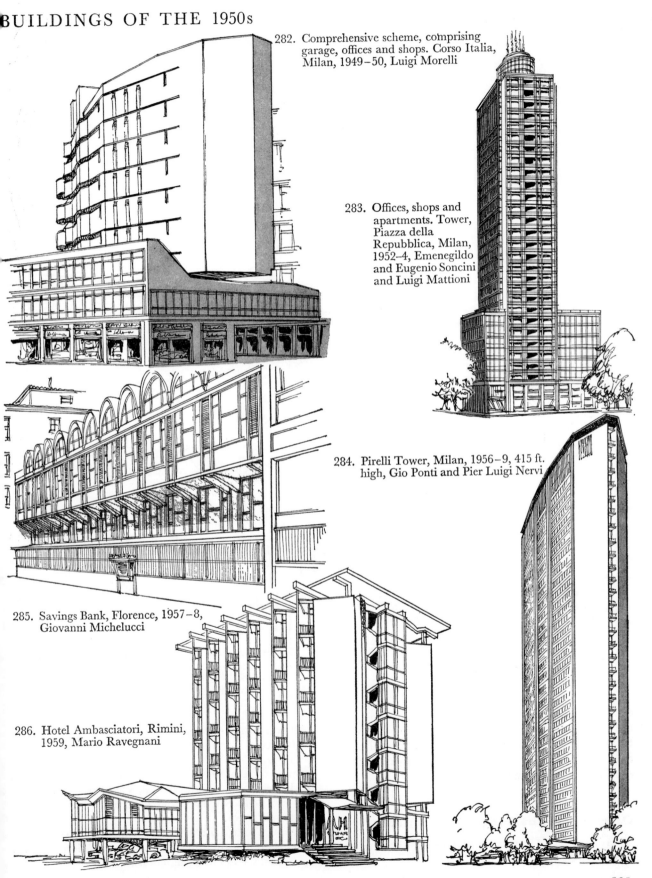

282. Comprehensive scheme, comprising garage, offices and shops. Corso Italia, Milan, 1949–50, Luigi Morelli

283. Offices, shops and apartments. Tower, Piazza della Repubblica, Milan, 1952–4, Emenegildo and Eugenio Soncini and Luigi Mattioni

284. Pirelli Tower, Milan, 1956–9, 415 ft. high, Gio Ponti and Pier Luigi Nervi

285. Savings Bank, Florence, 1957–8, Giovanni Michelucci

286. Hotel Ambasciatori, Rimini, 1959, Mario Ravegnani

287. Church of S. Ildefonso, Milan, 1955,
Carlo de Carli

derivative. It would be hard for Italian architects to ignore their unique heritage and, why should they, when their modern work is so superior to that of other countries and most inspiring?

Other notable buildings of the period

Agip Holiday Centre for Children, Cesenatico, Vaccaro, 1937–8.

Albergo Duomo, Milan, Bega, 1950s.
Biblioteca Comunale, Milan, Parisi and Longhi, 1950s.
Fiumicino Intercontinental Airport, Rome, Ligini, Luccichenti, Nervi, Ortensi, Vaccaro, 1957.
Museo della Scienza e della Tecnica, Milan, Portaluppi, 1950s.
School, Parco Lambro, Milan, de Carli, 1950.
Shops and swimming pool layout, Salsomaggisore 1960s, Clerici and Vignano.

Select Bibliography

All titles published in London unless otherwise stated.

Allsopp, B., *A History of Classical Architecture* (Pitman, 1965. Pitman, N.Y., 1966).

Archittetura di Eugenio Faludi, The Faludi Office, Italy.

Bardeschi, M. D., *Italian Villas Today* (Alec Tiranti, 1966. Transatlantic Press N.Y.).

Bossert, H. Th., and Zschietzschmann, W., *Hellas and Rome* (Zwemmer, 1936).

Briggs, M. S., *Architecture of Italy* (Dent).

Brion, M., and Smith, E., *Pompeii and Herculaneum* (Elek, 1960. Crown, N.Y.).

Busch, H., and Lohse, B., *Buildings of Europe series; Romanesque Europe*, 1960, *Gothic Europe*, 1959, *Renaissance Europe*, 1961, *Baroque Europe*, 1962. (Batsford. Macmillan, N.Y.).

Cichy, Dr. Bodo., *Architektur und Baustile* (Thorma, Munich, 1959).

Conant, K. J., *Carolingian and Romanesque Architecture 800–1200* (Pelican History of Art, 1959. Penguin, N.Y., 1967).

Copplestone, T., *World Architecture* (Paul Hamlyn, 1963).

Fletcher, Sir Banister, *A History of Architecture on the Comparative Method* (Athlone Press, 1960. Scribner, N.Y., 1961).

Franck, C. L., *The Villas of Frascati* (Alec Tiranti, 1966. Transatlantic, N.Y.).

Franklin, J. W., *The Cathedrals of Italy* (Batsford, 1958).

Galardi, A., *New Italian Architecture* (Architectural Press, 1967. Praeger, N.Y., 1967).

Grimal, P., *Rome of the Caesars* (Phaidon Press).

Gromort, G., *L'Architecture en Grèce et à Rome* (Vincent, Fréal, Paris, 1947).

Guida dell'Architettura Contemporarea in Roma (National Association of Italian Engineers and Architects, 1965) Italy.

Hamilton, J. A., *Byzantine Architecture and Decoration* (Batsford, 1956).

Harvey, J., *The Gothic World* (Batsford, 1950. Harper & Row, N.Y., 1969).

Hatje, G., *Encyclopaedia of Modern Architecture* (Thames and Hudson, 1963. Abrams, N.Y., 1964).

Hitchcock, H. R., *Architecture of the 19th and 20th Centuries* (Pelican History of Art, 1958. Penguin, N.Y., 1963).

Hughes, J. Q., and Lynton, N., *Renaissance Architecture* (Longmans Green, 1962. McKay, N.Y.).

Joedicke, J., *Pier Luigi Nervi* (Edizione di Communità, Milan, 1957).

Kidder-Smith, G. E., *The New Architecture of Europe* (Penguin, 1962).

Kidder-Smith, G. E., *New Churches of Europe* (Architectural Press, 1964. Holt, Rinehart & Winston, N.Y.).

Kidder-Smith, G. E., *Italy Builds* (Architectural Press, 1955).

Krautheimer, R., *Early Christian and Byzantine Architecture* (Pelican History of Art, 1965. Penguin, N.Y.).

Labò, M., *Giuseppe Terragni* (Il Balcone, Milan, 1947).

Lees-Milne, J., *Baroque Italy* (Batsford, 1959).

Melograni, C., *Giuseppe Pagano* (Il Balcone, Milan, 1955).

Milano Oggi (Milano Moderna, Milan, 1958).

Minoletti (Milano Moderna, Milan, 1959).

Murray, P. J., *The Architecture of the Italian Renaissance* (Batsford, 1963. Schocken, N.Y.).

Nervi, P. L., *New Structures* (Architectural Press, 1963), *Buildings, Projects Structures 1953–63* (Praeger, N.Y., 1963).

Pagani, C., *Architettura Italiana Oggi* (Ulrico Hoepli, Milan, 1955).

Pevsner, Prof. N., *An Outline of European Architecture* (Penguin Books, 1961).

Pica, A., *Recent Italian Architecture* (Edizione del Milione, Milan, 1959).

Plommer, H., *Ancient and Classical Architecture* (Longmans Green. McKay, N.Y.).

Sharp, M., *A Traveller's Guide to the Churches of Rome* (Hugh Evelyn, 1967). *Guide to the Churches of Rome* (Chilton, N.Y., 1967).

Stewart, C., *Early Christian, Byzantine and Romanesque Architecture* (Longmans Green. McKay, N.Y.).

Stewart, C., *Byzantine Legacy* (Allen and Unwin, 1947. Fernhill, N.Y., 1959).

West, T. W., *A History of Achitecture in Italy* (University of London Press, 1968. McKay, N.Y., 1969).

White, J., *Art and Architecture in Italy 1250–1400* (Pelican History of Art, 1966. Penguin, N.Y.).

Wittkower, R., *Art and Architecture in Italy 1600–1750* (Pelican History of Art, 1965. Penguin, N.Y., 1958).

Wittkower, R., *Gian Lorenzo Bernini* (Phaidon Press, 1955).

Glossary

The reference figures in brackets refer to line drawings throughout the book.

Abacus–The top member of a capital, usually a square or curved-sided slab of stone or marble (7).

Acanthus–A leaf form used in classical ornament (21).

Acropolis–A city on a hill. A Greek term usually implying also some fortification.

Agora–A Greek term for an open air place of assembly, generally the market place.

Ambulatory–A passage or aisle giving access between the choir with high altar and the apse of a church.

Anthemion–A type of classical ornament based on the honeysuckle flower (19).

Apse–Semi-circular or polygonal termination to a church, most commonly to be found on the eastern or transeptal elevations (126).

Arcade–A series of arches open, or closed with masonry, supported on columns or piers (120).

Architrave–The lowest member of the entablature (7).

Arcuated construction–Wherein the structure is supported on arches (43).

Arris–The vertical sharp edges between the flutes in a column (7).

Articulation–The designing defining and dividing up of a façade into vertical and horizontal architectural members.

Astragal–A moulding at the top of the column and below the capital.

Astylar–A classical façade without columns or pilasters (183).

Atrium–An entrance court in Roman houses but in Early Christian and Byzantine architecture, an open square or courtyard in front of the entrance (108).

Baldacchino–A canopy supported on pillars set over an altar or throne.

Barrel vault–A continuous vault in semi-circular section, like a tunnel (187).

Caldarium–The hot room in a Roman Baths.

Capital–The crowning feature of a column or pilaster (7).

Cella–The enclosed, central part of a Roman temple (55).

Centering–A structure, usually made of timber, set up to support a dome, vault or ceiling until construction is complete.

Clerestory–The upper storey in a church, generally pierced by a row of windows (76).

Coffer–Panel or caisson sunk into a ceiling, dome or vault. Often ornamented (52).

Corbel table–A projecting section of wall supported on corbels (carved blocks of stone or wood) and generally forming a parapet.

Cornice–The crowning member of the classical entablature (7).

Cruciform–A plan based on the form of a cross (189).

Dentil–Classical form of ornament.

Domical vault–A vault covering a square or polygonal compartment and shaped like a dome (112).

Dosseret–A deep block often placed above the Byzantine capital to support the wide voussoirs of the arch above (92).

Drum–The circular or polygonal-sided vertical walling supporting a dome (190).

Echinus–A curved, moulded member supporting the abacus of the Doric Order. The term is derived from the Greek *echinos* meaning sea urchin. The curve resembles the shell of the sea urchin (7).

Entablature–The horizontal member in classical architecture. It is subdivided into cornice, frieze and architrave (7).

Entasis–(7). See full definition in the note at the foot of page 11.

Fillet–A narrow flat band which divides mouldings from one another, also separates column flutes (14).

Flute–Vertical channelling in the shaft of a column (7).

Forum–The Roman place of assembly for markets, courts of justice and business.

Frieze–The central member of the classical entablature (7).

Greek cross plan–A cruciform plan where the four arms of the cross are of equal length (99).

Guilloche–Classical ornament in the form of an intertwined plait (9).

Guttae–Small cones under the mutules and triglyphs of the Doric entablature (7).

Hypocaust–A hollow space under the floor in which heat from the furnace was accumulated for warming rooms and hot water system. Used in Ancient Rome.

Intersecting vault–Where two vaults, either of semi-circular barrel section, or of pointed form, meet and intersect one another at right angles. Most usual instance is in the crossing of a church where the transepts cross the nave and choir.

Key pattern–Classical ornament (9).

Lantern–Structure for ventilation and light. Often surmounting a dome or tower (242).

Latin cross plan–A cruciform plan where the nave is longer than the other three arms (140).

Lintel–The horizontal stone slab or timber beam spanning an opening and supported on columns or walls.

Metope–The space between the triglyphs of a Doric frieze. Often decorated with sculptured groups or carved ornament (7).

Module–A unit of measurement based on proportion by which the parts of a classical order are regulated. Generally taken from the half-diameter of the column at its junction with the base. In modern architecture, a standard unit adopted for convenience of mass production.

Monolithic column–One whose shaft is of one piece of stone or marble in contrast to one made up in hollow drums.

Mutule–Blocks attached under Doric cornices from which the guttae depend (7).

Naos–Chamber in a Greek temple containing the cult statue (25).

Narthex–The western portico or ante-nave in Early Christian and Byzantine churches railed off for women and penitents (98).

Necking–The space between the astragal of the column shaft and the actual capital (23).

Orchestra–Space where the chorus danced and sang in a Greek theatre (29).

Pediment–The triangular feature in classical architecture which resembles the Gothic gable. Supported on the entablature over porticoes, windows and doors (7).

Pendentive–Spherical triangles formed by the intersecting of the dome by two pairs of opposite arches themselves carried on four piers or columns (see pages 36–7).

Peristyle–A row of columns surrounding a temple, court or cloister also the space so enclosed (24).

Piano nobile–An Italian Renaissance term meaning literally the 'noble floor'. In classical building it is the first and principal floor of a house.

Pilaster–A column of rectangular section, often engaged in the wall (67).

Pilaster strip–Low relief vertical strips with the appearance of pilasters but with only decorative not constructional purpose.

Plateresque–A form of rich surface ornament in Spanish architecture used in both Gothic and Renaissance buildings. The term is derived from *plateria* = silverwork.

Podium–A continuous projecting base or pedestal (54).

Pozzolana–See page 18.

Rustication–A treatment of masonry with sunk joints and roughened surfaces. Used in classical architecture (166).

Set-off–Sloping or horizontal member connecting the lower and thicker part of a wall with the receding upper part.

Shaft–The column of an order, between the capital and the base (7).

Squinch–Arches placed diagonally across the internal angles of a tower or base of drum to convert the square form into an octagonal base to support an octagonal spire or a circular drum (page 36).

Stylobate–A basement, generally of three steps, supporting a row of columns in Greek temple design (7).

Tepidarium–Room of moderate heat in a Roman Baths.

Trabeated construction–A structure composed of horizontal lintels and vertical posts as in Greek architecture (26).

Transept–The arms of a cruciform plan church set at right angles to the nave and choir. Transepts are generally aligned north to south.

Travertine–An Italian building stone of a porous, yellowish type.

Triforium–The central, or first floor stage, of a medieval church between the nave arcade and the clerestory. The triforium is usually arcaded and may have a passage behind at first floor level extending continuously round the church.

Triglyph–The blocks, cut with vertical channels, which are set at regular intervals in the frieze of the Doric Order (7).

Tympanum–The triangular space between the sloping and horizontal cornices of a classical pediment, also, in Medieval buildings, the space between the lintel and arch of a doorway (7).

Volute–A spiral or scroll to be seen in Ionic, Corinthian and Composite capitals (23).

Voussoir–The wedge-shaped stones which compose an arch (30).

INDEX

Page references are printed in ordinary type; illustration references in **heavy type.**